Let's Band Together

Christopher H Northey-Youngs

Cover design and artwork by Christopher H Northey-Youngs

Copyright © 2023 Christopher H Northey-Youngs

All rights reserved.

ISBN:9798377782292

DEDICATION

I am pleased to dedicate this book to my piano teacher, Ann Tate, who introduced me to a world of musical wonder at an early age, and also, to my trumpet teacher, Frank Huxham, who showed me how much fun blowing into a piece of metal pipe can be!

Contents

Page			
3	Prologue	-	Who Is This Book For?
5	Chapter 1	-	The Industrial Revolution
15	Chapter 2	-	Victorian Pride
25	Chapter 3	-	Rebirth - The Post-War Years
33	Chapter 4	-	Roll on the Seventies
43	Chapter 5	-	Happy Banding 1980 - 1990
63	Chapter 6	-	Tavistock Carnival
75	Chapter 7	-	Entente Cordiale
83	Chapter 8	-	Centenary Celebrations
89	Chapter 9	-	Bugle Contest
97	Chapter 10	-	Building a Band of Ability
102	Chapter 11	-	The Glory of Contesting
117	Chapter 12	-	Troubled Times
120	Chapter 13	-	Denzil Stephens
124	Chapter 14	-	The Bristol Contest
134	Chapter 15	-	The Snowball Effect
137	Chapter 16	-	The Proms Project
141	Chapter 17	-	Tavistock Pro Brass
145	Chapter 18	-	Tavistock Versatile Brass Ensemble
159	Chapter 19	-	Concentrating on Making Music
178	Chapter 20	-	Tavistock Rhythm & Brass
187	Chapter 21	-	Conclusion
193	Final Note	-	Abaddons Not Telling
195	Foot Note	-	Who Is Abaddon?

ACKNOWLEDGMENTS

My thanks to Julia Chalmers for her photographic skills, and for being there to capture the fun we had at our Sterts Theatre Concerts and also the Christmas caroling events. Special thanks to my Sixth Form Tutor and History Teacher, Gerry Woodcock, who instilled in me a love of local history and for his help with researching chapter two. Also, many thanks to Becky Frisby, for her help in trying to help improve my poor English and punctuation. Many thanks to all my 'brass banding' friends past and present, and to those who supplied memories, photos, and stories, in particular to Brian Routledge, Peter & Margaret Hurdwell, Ruth Memory and Rachel Hutty. And finally, as always, to my husband, Martin for his ongoing support, love and affection.

Prologue

You may be wondering, who is this book for? Is it for people who like to learn about the history of an organisation? Or perhaps, for people who want to find out more about Brass Bands and what is now a worldwide musical movement? Is it just for those Brass Banding types? Those people who get excited over, and can talk for hours about the latest redesign of the cornet mouthpiece, or what happened all those years ago at the Area competitions? The people who don't bother putting things on the kitchen calendar, and then announce on the Friday that you're all off to play at some bandstand in a place you have never heard of the following day?

Well, yes and no. Those types are, no doubt, going to find this story interesting, and be able to draw parallels between the words recorded here and their own life experiences, but, the main learning's here are for anyone and everyone, at least anyone who has socialised with like-minded people in groups, people who share a common interest, anyone who has found friendship in a club or society and anyone who has mixed with other people with a similar goal or objective.

Even if you have managed not to get drawn onto that club or society committee, if you have been a member of such an organisation, you will have no doubt been affected by their decisions and choices. Best case scenario is that you gain enjoyment and pleasure from your mixing with this group of people, and you gain a purpose and friends for life. Worst case scenario, things don't go to plan and so called 'friends' end up 'putting a spanner in the works'. Sometimes, you fail to see what is clearly in plain sight, and that some people can't help but have a negative or destructive nature to them, those people who might be called the 'wolves in sheep's clothing', those who we will call Abaddon.

Perhaps, consider these questions;

- Why do brass bands often suffer so badly from politics?

- Is there more to brass bands than I originally thought?

- What can I learn from this cautionary social tale?

- How can I ensure my social group gets on and avoids self-destruction?

- And who is Abaddon?

If that has, even remotely, managed to spark your interest - then read on, and we'll find even with the best intentions, it's not always easy to succeed in '**Banding Together.**'

Chapter 1 – The Industrial Revolution

"To join the industrial revolution, you needed to open a factory; in the internet revolution, you need to open a laptop." – **Alexis Ohanian** - *American internet entrepreneur and co-founder of Reddit*

If you are a musician and have never played in a Brass Band, some would say you have missed out, for it is true that 'banding' can bring a sense of great camaraderie, friendship and a feeling of self-worth. The benefits of effective teamwork can indeed reap the rewards of musical success and personal happiness. But then again, others might say you have saved yourself a lot of stress, sadness and heartache, by avoiding continual bickering, back-biting and the never-ending doom of politics which resides so firmly in the world of brass bands. Be clear from the start that being a part of any such musical team can be fraught, as it comes with both extreme happiness and sadness in equal measure. It's a sharp two-edged sword that can stab you right in the heart, inflicting a wound that sometimes even a lifetime is not long enough for it to heal.

It is well documented that Brass bands came into being with the working classes back in the 19th century. Due to the development of the Industrial Revolution, new thriving communities based around local industry were created. Many small villages became towns, and large towns became cities. Large factories and investment in new housing for workers and general infrastructure greatly increased the populations which came together to earn a living in the new metropolises which grew up around such massive industries. The UK was seen as the 'workshop' of the world. The development of the steam engine was to revolutionise manufacturing, communication and transportation. The businessmen were leaders in international commerce and banking, trade and shipping. The growing British Empire also brought some better working conditions and increased living standards meant even the lower classes had a chance to see themselves as aspiring to be better than their parents. After a hard day's work people would enjoy socialising, having a few beers with their workmates and then coming together to make music playing in their brass band. This was often as close to 'the arts' as they would ever get. Many people rarely travelled very far from home and opportunities for relief from the grind of daily life were few and far between, to say the least.

The development of the piston valve made the production of brass instruments accessible to even the average person, especially with the support of business and factory proprietors who sought to continue the education of its employees. Certainly, industries were especially proud to have their own brass bands to further promote their business names. Coal mines, collieries, mills and certain heavy industry led the way in promoting the growing popularity of brass bands amongst the working classes. At this time, it also acted as a way for employers to occupy the leisure time of workers which kept them away from their preoccupation with political activities. Being part of a band was open to anyone, well, as long as you were male. The local brass band helped to generate a sense of civic pride in local communities. By the 1850s playing in competitions and competing against the neighbouring brass band provided people with a sense of solidarity and achievement and fuelled their desire to see themselves as being better than the next town's band.

In 1853 the first brass band British Open Championships were held in Manchester. The event saw a crowd of over 16,000 people and with cash prizes for the winning bands, I'm sure it was a staunchly fought competition. Businessmen and entrepreneurs promoted the competitions and entry for listeners would have been free or at least affordable for the working-class supporters. Today two major championships are held each year in England; the National Championships and the British Open Championship. The National Championship is only open to bands from England, Scotland and Wales. It is recorded that this competition ran sporadically between 1856 and 1900 when it was firmly established by G&S impresario Sir Arthur Sullivan in 1900. The Open Championship invites bands from all countries and has been in existence since 1853, the first winners being 'Mossley Temperance Saxhorn Band.'

Brass bands were at their peak in the 1890s with over 5,000 bands in the country. The figure today stands around 1,200, with around 30,000 players. You might ask why the decline in the number of brass bands? Many bands survived by being attached to certain industries such as mining and the textile industry. But as these industries declined, so did the financial support for their brass band. Also, as we have recently found following Covid-19 and the various 'lockdowns' many people simply found other interests and uses for their time.

Like today, with each generation comes the opportunity to pursue other ways of occupying their ever-increasing amount of free time. Why go out and join a community group when you have the world in the palm of your hand with a smartphone? If you have ever heard your parents say "it wasn't like this in my day" then prepare yourself, as you will no doubt be using that phrase at some point in your future. After all, we all turn into our parents, right?

Me with the British Open Championship Shield.

There are, however many non-contesting bands who merely seek to provide entertainment for audiences and enjoyment for musicians. From time to time they might make a foray into the world of brass band competitions to be judged by one person sat blind in a tent in the middle of the concert arena. But much happiness is still to be found playing a varied programme of music just for fun rather than concentrating on practising one piece of music for weeks on end, with the conductor becoming ever more upset that, even though he has asked one hundred times already, "you are still not playing that section quiet enough." Following the competition these pieces of music rarely warrant inclusion in your basic 'Summer Programme', instead they are returned to the music library often never to see the light of day again. I can recall many times sitting in the rehearsal room following a competition to listen to 'the people who know about these things' proclaim "That adjudicator is an expert and knows what he is talking about". Then in other bands that, perhaps, did not do so well say "That adjudicator! He's an idiot who doesn't have a clue what he's talking about". It's the risk you take entering such a lottery. Some days you'll have a good day, and other times you won't, but after all, it's only one person's opinion, a fact many people find so difficult to grasp.

We must remember that even a band made up of brilliant musicians can fail if they are not able to play cohesively. They must pay attention to the detail and information found on the page, the 'louds and softs' while keeping an eye on the Conductor who is responsible for keeping everyone on track with regard to tempo and musical interpretation. However, do not mistake a conductor as being merely a metronome. You only have to watch a top section brass band to see that the conductor very rarely just beats time. He is the Maestro, the shaper, the music maker. He paints tones and colour in music through his baton and arms.

There is also the problem of intonation, the bane of many a fourth section brass band. Blowing into a brass instrument using a mouthpiece to start a vibrating stream of air will produce a sound. The shorter the length of metal tube then the higher the pitch of the resulting note. The longer the tube the lower the note that will sound, hence the smaller cornet will sound higher than the larger tuba. Throw in a mix of varied tube lengths with instruments such as tenor horns, baritone horns and euphoniums, then you can produce a whole range of notes that when played together can produce a variety of musical sounds. Most brass band instruments are conical in shape which produces a more mellow sound. While blowing your instrument can produce a note, the movement of the lips on the mouthpiece can also vary the pitch of the note produced. This is known as 'intonation' and should not be confused with the word tuning. Really bad sounds can be the result of bad intonation. This is particularly noticeable if players are supposed to be playing the same note. If one or more player is even slightly sharp or flat [higher or lower in pitch] than the others, then a sort of dissonance is heard. This is often the downfall of many a lower section contesting band. The nerves and shakes caused by sitting on a large stage in front of your peers, a large audience and not to mention the adjudicator can often cause the best intentions of maintaining good intonation to go out of the window. Have you ever seen a conductor point to his ears during a performance? Standing out the front they can hear if players are blowing their notes too sharp or flat and that some sort of adjustment is needed.

How often have you heard the phrase "there is no I in team!"? Let's remind ourselves of the dictionary definition of 'Band' – 'a group of people who share the same interests or beliefs; or have joined together for a specific purpose.' If your group all have the same goal of making great music, having fun, and enjoying the company of others, while being able to accept that not all people have the same musical ability as you, then your banding will bring you harmony and happiness. This will no doubt improve your well-being, both mentally and physically. If not, then you will be on a rocky road of discord and you'll find yourself in more of a disbanded band than a band.

In the following pages, I have tried to document the trials and tribulations, the ups and downs of a long-standing brass band based in the market town of Tavistock, on the Devon, Cornwall border, from its humble beginnings, through to its glory days and finally to its ultimate unfortunate demise.

I was brought up on an isolated farm on the outskirts of the town of Tavistock in the late 1960s and 1970s, and other than my parents and three brothers I was given little opportunity to mix with other people. I was constantly reminded by my parents and those scary public information films on the TV, that farms were indeed deadly places.

Me sat on the tractor next to my Dad with my two older brothers.

Although I did have my two older brothers, Malcolm and Graham, and also my younger brother Roger, the possibility of having school friends and other kids around to play and have fun with was simply not an option. I know now that lots of kids would have loved to have been brought up on a farm, with all the animals, nature and hundreds of acres of land to explore, but as with most young people, you are perhaps not aware of how lucky you are.

From an early age I enjoyed bashing our tunes on the family piano so much, that my parents encouraged me to have piano lessons. So from an age of about seven, every Monday I would enjoy an escape from the farm to have piano lessons with a lovely lady called Ann Tait, in Lewdown, some 10 miles north of Tavistock. As my interest in music grew, I learnt of a neighbour who lived in one of the cottages about half a mile down the lane, who had recently joined a newly reformed brass band in the town. They practised every Sunday morning, and he offered to give me a lift to a rehearsal to see if I would like to join. So, aged only about 9 or 10, I walked the mile to his house, and we set off into the town. I was handed a rickety old cornet and simply by taking it into my hands, by default I joined Tavistock Town Band. At that time, I was not aware of the band's rich history, nor did I know that in time I was destined to become part of it.

Being a so-called 'creative' I'm not known for my writing skills, and I have never managed to write anything approaching thirty three thousand words on any topic in my life. So, to challenge myself, I needed to write about something that meant a lot to me, something that I had a passion for, something that had already taken up over forty years of my life. So, sit back and listen to my tales of cheese and onion sandwiches, wobbly chairs, secret compartments, royal visits, a town that played its part in the 'D-Day landings' and of friendships made and lost, but mainly of banding found, maintained, transformed and ultimately, sadly taken away.

A rare photo of me and my dad taken a few years before he passed away in 2018.

Although my Dad had a terrific sense of humour, and enjoyed a long life into his 90s, he was not someone who shared my pastime or love of music, he had his own interests.

Chapter 2 – Victorian Pride

"When life seems hard, the courageous do not lie down and accept defeat: instead, they are all the more determined to struggle for a better future." - **Queen Victoria**

Everything starts somewhere and our story of Tavistock Town Band started with a certain gentleman called George Williams, a Tavistock insurance agent. He operated his business from his home in West Street, Tavistock. In 1890 he was one of the founding members of the Mercantile Association, a body set up to promote the town's trade. At that time, in the absence of an effective local council, the Association saw itself as representing the interests of Tavistock in a wider sense, and when Williams became its president in 1897, he found himself campaigning on a wide range of issues. Of the initiatives that bore fruit, one was the formation, in the same year, of the Tavistock Town Band.

There had, of course, been a good deal of instrumental music-making in the town before 1897. In 1849, for example, a locally recruited band was in attendance when the Tavistock Cottage Garden Society held its second annual exhibition at the Bedford Hotel. The musicians on that occasion, it was reported, "added much to the pleasurable feelings of their audience by their superior playing". The next decade or so saw the establishment of many other local bands. The competition between them helped to raise standards. That was the view of at least one correspondent of the Tavistock Gazette in 1863, who wrote "For some time past our town has been highly favoured in the pleasure resulting from the performances of well-trained bands of musicians. Bands have sprung up, and have made good progress, increasing the enjoyment of the public, who in return have regarded them with hearty approval. It has been a pleasure to spend an hour on a Saturday night in the square or the streets listening to these bands". The rivalries that developed did have some unfortunate consequences. To attract interest and support, bands tended to play outdoors as much as possible, and incidents occasionally arose. In one case, the Band of Hope Band, whilst playing in the street one summer evening, was twice "ambushed" by another band intent on stopping them playing. "Dirt", it was reported, "was thrown". There was also a steady stream of complaints about the concerts going on late into the night.

Tavistock Salvation Army Band [perhaps] 1920.

The Band of Hope Band was the earliest example of a band whose primary concern was to promote a church's interest. The tradition was later maintained, and strengthened, by the local Salvation Army Band. There were various other bands associated with other town organisations. In the 1860s there was the Fife and Drum Band of the Mechanics'

Institute. In 1859 the band attached to the local Rifle Volunteer Corps was founded. In the 1880s they were chosen to play at the opening of the swimming baths in Bannawell Street, the unveiling of the original Sir Francis Drake statue at the end of Plymouth Road and Queen Victoria's Golden Jubilee Celebrations.

Early photo of Tavistock Town Band – date unknown.

From 1864 the various bands were able to use the newly-opened Town Hall. But the bulk of their music-making remained outdoors, either in the streets, or at organised events such as fetes, sporting events, or civic occasions. Bedford Square, which was a wide open space in front of the Town Hall, remained the most popular venue for summer evening concerts and musical accompaniment became an essential feature of annual events like Whit Monday at The Ring and Christmas Day in the Workhouse.

Despite the plethora of local bands that existed in the last half of the nineteenth century, there remained, according to Mr Williams and his colleagues, a gap to be filled. They felt that the existence of a Town Band was a question of civic pride. Subscribers were recruited and instruments bought, and in 1897, a new band was formed that called itself "The Tavistock Brass Band". A committee was formed, with Henry Gaud, the proprietor of the Queen's Head, as secretary, and John Tomlinson, a music teacher and organist, who lived in Watts Road, was appointed as conductor.

But, unfortunately, the project soon ran into trouble. There were some charges that the administration was slack, and that committee members were not being given enough notice of meetings. Debit balances began to appear in the accounts, and the rumour that this was the result of bandsmen receiving free drinks at the Queen's Head Hotel after band practices was hotly denied. In 1900 an opposition band was launched amid stories that the Town Band was facing collapse.

In 1901 Messrs Williams, Gaud, and Tomlinson, amid a welter of recrimination, had to consider selling off the instruments to pay the bills. They managed to keep going for some time, and in 1907 played at a series of open-air concerts in Bank Square and Bedford Square. But by 1912 it was over. In the Minutes of the Tavistock Hospital Committee for August of that year, it was noted that the hospital had received £6 from Mr C.F. Green, "being part of the proceedings from the sale of band instruments belonging to the Tavistock Band". Charles Green was a local coal merchant and presumably, he was the band's treasurer. It was to be 25 years before a revival of the Town Band was attempted.

Tavistock's Victorian Town Hall – the venue for many a band concert.

In October 1937, William Barkell, the Chairman of the Urban District Council and Duke Street tobacconist called a public meeting to test opinion on the possibility of forming a new Town Band. A few years before, the Volunteer Corps Band had folded along with many others, leaving only the band of the Salvation Army. Of the Town Band that had been established in 1897 nothing was said, one speaker declaring, without contradiction, that there never had been one. There was a feeling among the seventy people present that the town was big enough to sustain and support a new town brass band and that the recently-erected bandstand in the Meadows should be put to use. It was decided to open a subscription list, and to ask the Chairman of the Council to be the ex-officio President of the new enterprise.

Over the years, the Council was to play an important role in bridging the gaps between the band's 'active periods'.

Mr N.S.G. Mallett was appointed as Secretary and Sidney Berry, manager of the local branch of the Midland Bank, became Treasurer. It was almost a year before the inaugural concert was held. On September 28th, 1938, the new band played in public for the first time, in the Town Hall. Starting with Greenwood's "The Pirate Prince", and ending with Rimmer's "Our Glorious Empire", they played a programme that included not only marches, but operatic selections and ballads, and featured, in the middle, Master J Neri on piano and Master P Neri on cornet. It was, perhaps, an evening when some minds might have been on other things, as the following morning, Prime Minister Neville Chamberlain flew off to meet Hitler at Munich.

West Street Tavistock – the Queen's Head pub is down the hill on the left [now a Wetherspoons], and the Cornish Arms is down the hill on the right.

The new enterprise seemed to be dogged by controversy from the outset. An invitation to accompany a British Legion parade out to Kelly College was first accepted and then rejected when it became known that a Plymouth band had been engaged to play at the service in the college. Then there developed a rift between the Band Committee and a Band Supporters' Club that had been established in February 1938 to help fund the venture. Acrimonious exchanges included charges of the 'tail wagging the dog, led to the Club's decision in July 1939, to disband. The band continued to operate, using a room at the Cornish Arms as its headquarters. Under the baton of Mr C Trewin they played at a variety of functions throughout the summer. On the last Saturday in August, they took themselves off in two motor coaches, for a day's outing to St Austell. A week later it was announced that owing to "the crisis", the band had decided to suspend its practices for the time being. Within a week more than half of the players had joined the forces as Britain was drawn into the World War II. The instruments were collected by the Band Sergeant, Mr Gloyn, and were then deposited in the Council basement for safekeeping.

I must credit my old history teacher and sixth form tutor Gerry Woodcock for his help in getting started on this chapter. Although he has now sadly passed away, his knowledge of the history of the town of Tavistock was extensive and his ability to enthuse his students to take an interest in history certainly rubbed off on me. Thanks Gerry.

Some pictures of my Mum. She always had a great sense of fun and encouraged my music making, but often found it difficult to show any affection in any type of physical way.

If you visit Tavistock, be sure to take the short-cut down to the Town via 'Madge' Lane. All thirty three steps on the way up will prove invaluable exercise.

Also, seek out 'Betsy Grimbal's' tower, part of the remains of the Benedictine Abbey, and see if you can spot the stone sarcophagus which lies inside.

Take a trip through the park [the Meadows] and see if you can find the paddling pool outline in the grass, now sadly loss having been filled in by an over conscientious council in the early 1980s.

Chapter 3 – Rebirth - The Post-War Years

"Do not judge me by my successes, judge me by how many times I fell down and got back up again." – **Nelson Mandela** – *South African anti-apartheid activist and politician.*

The Band's Chairman (1997 – 2000), Brian Routledge, has helped provide information covering the post-war re-launch of the band which came in 1946. The Band reformed under the baton of Herbert Eke. The help of the Council was requested, and this resulted in the band using the District Council offices in Pym Street for practices. The building today is 'Drake's Wine Bar & Café' having previously been 'The Ordulph Arms' pub. Brian recalls progress was slow to start with, but in 1947, a rift occurred in the local Salvation Army Band which resulted in the band gaining five very proficient players which helped tremendously. It appeared that 'fall-outs' and politics could have their benefits too.

Note the wooden name shield in the front, here in this 1940s photo.

As an aside, on the topic of 'fall-outs', I was once told a story of a band in the Cornish town of Bude [Bude Town Band] which was struck a particularly difficult blow [excuse the pun] when problems arose with a whole family of players in 2003. The family's surname was 'Inch' and when the family left en-bloc, a new brass band was formed called Bude Metric Brass. When I asked why they called themselves 'Metric Brass' I was told they chose that name "because there were no 'Inches' in it." However, if you peruse their website it says the band was originally conceived as a ten piece ensemble – hence the name 'Metric'.

The new Tavistock Town Band gave its first concert in 1947 in the Town Hall. The upstairs large hall with its Victorian vaulted ceiling, polished wood floor and walls adorned with portraits of the town's rich and famous past is still the same today. It seats around 400 people. Brian recalls the hall was packed with people as the concert had received good local publicity and press coverage. The band's solo cornet player at that time was Bill Smale; but for some reason, the Musical Director, Mr Eke decided that a 13-year old young Brian would play a solo for this concert. Who would have thought that on that concert night in 1947, that same young lad would go on to become the band's Chairman some fifty years later?

Brian Routledge in his Tavistock Town Band uniform.

The band had three main objectives: - to get larger practice rooms, to take part in competitions and contests, and to buy a set of uniforms. The first aim was soon achieved thanks to the Army and Regimental Sergeant, and Major Drake who made the drill hall at Rocky Hill available for the band's practices.

The new band's first contest was in Exeter and although Herbert Eke was the band's conductor, the band enlisted the help of a Plymouth man to help prepare the band. Brian recalls the opening passage involved a cornet melody which required some considerable practice from the cornet section. At the contest, the band came second being beaten by only one point and the trophy was brought back to Tavistock where it was displayed in the window of Stan Willis' Butcher's shop at the bottom of West Street.

Tavistock Town Band after winning a cup for musical excellence c.1957
Band Conductor David Carthew is sat in the centre.

Fundraising was undertaken to buy uniforms. The Saturday night dances held in the Town Hall were very popular and profitable. In 1949/50, the band had raised enough and smart new uniforms were bought. The uniform colours were black jackets with crimson lapels and cuffs, together with bright gold braid on the shoulders. It also included a belt around the middle and black trousers with a red stripe down each leg and was finished off with a peaked cap. They were made of a very heavy material which proved to be very warm, especially at the mid-summer evening concerts on Looe seafront. My good friend Mike Cole can be seen here posing as a child with his brand-new uniform.

Mike Cole, as a child, posing in his new band uniform.

Herbert Eke like many others after him moved away from the area due to work commitments. It was now that the band obtained the services of David Carthew. David was an ex-Royal Marine and a fine saxophone and clarinet player. He was assisted by the Band's solo euphonium player Tom Craze. Unlike a modern band, at that time the majority of players were all local. The player who lived furthest away came from no further than the village of Gunnislake which is only a few miles outside of the town, just across the river Tamar which divides the counties of Devon and Cornwall.

The Band's Musical Director David Carthew meets the young Princess Elizabeth on her visit to Tavistock in 1949, three years before her Coronation and accession to the throne.

The Princess walks around the Guildhall Square outside Court Gate.

Tavistock Guildhall Square with the main gate to the Benedictine Abbey still present.

Court Gate is thought to have been one of the main entrances to the Benedictine Abbey which was formed in 974. The Abbey was later dissolved and destroyed by Henry VIII in 1539, although several remnants of the original buildings can still be found around the town. The land was given to John Russell, 1st Baron Russell who later became 1st Earl of Bedford in 1550. In 1694 the family received the titles of Marquess of Tavistock and Duke of Bedford and their descendants were responsible for erecting many of the 19th century public buildings and statues which remain today. For more information, regarding the rich history of the Town of Tavistock, check out the town's website www.tavistock.gov.uk

The band plays at Mary Tavy near Tavistock late 1940s/early 1950s.

By the early 1960s interest was again waning, and the bandmaster David Carthew, reported a lack of enthusiasm and an unwillingness to attend practices. In June 1964 the band was wound up and again the Town Council agreed to store the instruments, along with uniforms and money, pending a possible revival.

Remnants of Tavistock's Benedictine Abbey.

Chapter 4 – Roll on the Seventies

"I spent my childhood clad in 1970s hand-me-downs, primarily from male cousins, which mainly consisted of a selection of beige, brown and orange dungarees. That, combined with a perfectly round pudding-bowl haircut, made me look, on a good day, like a cross between Ann Widdecombe, one of the Flower Pot Men, and a monk." – **Miranda Hart** – *comedy actress*

The band reformed again in 1974/5, after an advertisement appeared in the local newspapers, the Tavistock Times and the Tavistock Gazette. The instruments and old music stored by the Town Council in a basement cupboard were retrieved and after much cleaning and repairs, some of the instruments were still playable. The new Musical Director was David Moore. He was a clarinet and saxophone player with the Royal Marines based in Plymouth. The band practised in a barn to the rear of the Queen's Head Hotel. Today, this is the back bar area in the 'Wetherspoons' pub of the same name.

Conductor David Moore stands before the band in the United Reformed Church Hall, Russell Street, Tavistock.

This picture was taken in the hall underneath Tavistock's United Reformed Church. Note the 'sign board' bottom left. It was taken, perhaps, a year before I joined the band and I can recognise quite of few of the faces shown, although I can't remember all of their names. Les Tucker is sat in the solo cornet position. Together with his brother Harry, they were long-standing members of the band. Treasurer, Heather Campbell, is sat behind the centre table. Ruth Down is standing towards the centre/back. She was my mentor as we later both played second cornet when the band moved its practice room to the Market Inn's stable block, more on that later. Andy Myers can be seen sat with his French horn and he later became the band's conductor. A few seats along I can see John Harms and Andy Clark. They were to become long-term members of the band on baritone horn and euphonium. Percussionist Doughy Young holds his drumsticks and my neighbour Steve Page sits at the side with his trombone. Steve was kind enough to give me a lift to the band for many years before I learnt to drive and got my first car.

Playing Christmas Carols in Bedford Square Tavistock early 1970s.

Another Musical Director named Keith Ballard, a postmaster from St. Ann's Chapel, also took the Band for a period in 1975 as his name is included on a programme for the City of Plymouth District Scout Council's Barbecue and Summer Fair. This was held at Blindmans Wood, Outland Road, Plymouth on Saturday 28th June 1975, and admission was the grand price of 3p.

The music played at this time was the old band's library of marches and classical adaptations from musicals such as 'Pirates of Penzance', 'Oliver' and a few newer pieces from recent TV programmes such as 'Eye Level' from the popular TV series 'Van der Valk'. I can also remember that a selection from the 'New Seekers' and the Beatles Medley brought a welcome relief from the older tunes. Other pieces such as 'Hootenanny', 'Paloma Blanca' and 'Swinging Safari' were to become regular favourites with the audiences, and to some players, [who yearn for new contemporary music] the bane of brass band music programmes, even today.

A Summer Fair programme from 1975 note the Admittance is only 3p

In 1978, the band gained a new Musical Director Andy Myers, a talented French horn player from Laira Youth Band in Plymouth. Although he was only 17 at the time, he was a very competent musician and he encouraged more young people to join, so slowly the band began to grow. The band moved its rehearsal room to a musty stable in the car park of the 'Mariner Inn', later renamed the 'Market Inn', on Whitchurch Road. The walls were whitewashed, and the floor consisted of cobblestones, so it was not only the music that was sometimes a little wobbly. There was no heating, and the stable doors allowed the wind to blow into the room. We had managed to get some old school chairs to sit on and I can remember that as the metal legs wobbled between the stones, it made a screeching sound as they scraped against the cobblestone floor. Within a few years, Andy Myers gained a place at Music College in London and we all said our goodbyes.

Andy Myers conducts a concert in the hall beneath Tavistock United Reformed Church.

There were not enough of the old uniforms to go around, and no one wanted to wear them as the material was thick and far too heavy, so the band chose a more laid-back and 1970's style. This can be seen in the photo on the previous page. A popular venue for our concerts was a hall beneath the United Reformed Church on Russell Street. The stage was small, but as we were only a small band everything worked well, especially the use of the kitchen at the back of the hall which provided a welcome cup of tea during the concert interval.

In the picture, to the left of the conductor is the bespectacled face of Harry Tucker, one of two prominent brothers who were key players in helping the band reform. Harry and Leslie Tucker both played the cornet and until June 1994. Leslie still played in the band. For many years he had been responsible for the tuition given to new and younger members of the band.

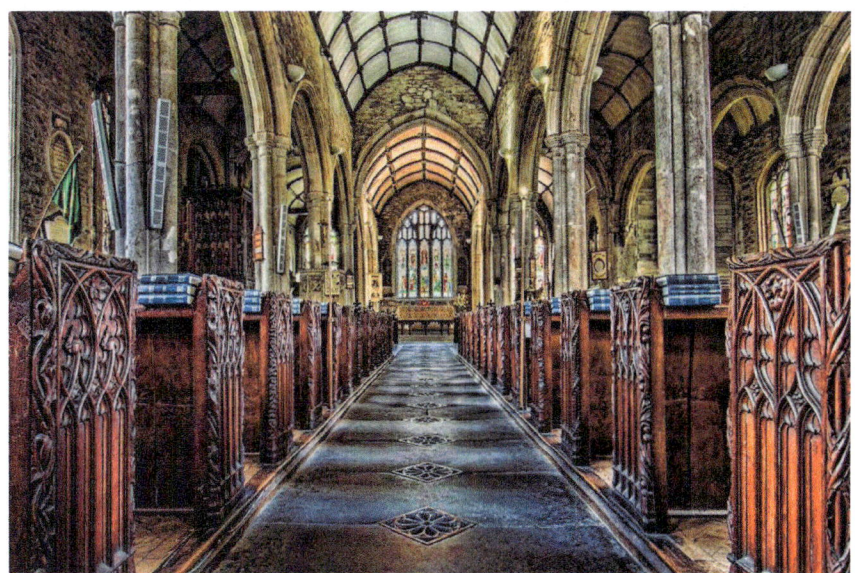

**Tavistock Parish Church – a later venue for our May annual concert
Credit to Tavistock's Mark Truman for such a great photo**

PROGRAMME

1.45 p.m. GATES OPEN
Musical Selection by
TAVISTOCK TOWN BAND
Bandmaster: Keith Ballard, Esq.

2.20 p.m. PARADE OF SCOUT COLOURS

2.30 p.m. GRAND OPENING CEREMONY
by
Councillor L. Hill, Esq., J.P.
Chairman Councillor E. J. Savery, Esq., MA, LIB.

2.45 p.m. TAVISTOCK TOWN BAND

3.30 p.m. DISPLAYS

4.30 p.m. TAVISTOCK TOWN BAND

6.30 p.m. GRAND SUMMER FAIR DRAW
(including PRIZE BINGO)

Headquarters: Main Hall

There will be a **Free Draw Prize** for those who are in the Hall during the Evening Main Draw and Prize Bingo.

We have a great variety of ....

STALLS — SIDESHOWS

DRAWS — COMPETITIONS

BINGO

ROASTING

Teas and Refreshments in comfort and at popular prices in the Main Headquarters Hall and in the Marquee on the top site.

ICE CREAM — HOT DOGS — MINERALS

SUPER STAMP STALL IN 7th PLYMOUTH H.Q.

BARBECUE BILL
will award a prize to the first person to challenge him with the words "you are Barbecue Bill".
(You must be carrying a programme)

SUMMER FAIR DRAW
with dozens of magnificent prizes
including

First Prize	...	...	£15
Second Prize	...	...	£10
Third Prize	...	...	£5

Tickets on sale during Fair

For a while, the band returned to premises it had occupied in 1939 and rehearsed in a room at the Cornish Arms. It was located at the back car park and was accessed by a narrow staircase. At the top of the staircase was a large white door with a covered peephole in it. This room was a meeting place for The Royal Antediluvian Order of Buffaloes (RAOB). They were a sort of Free Mason-type group, and they were happy for us to use their meeting room as a practice room. Later the band moved to the Day Care Centre at Abbey Rise on Whitchurch Road, in the centre of the town, and rehearsed every Sunday morning. Later, the band made its final move to the basement of the Town Council Offices in Drake Road where it remained until 2015.

For a couple of years, 1978 and 1979, various people took the baton. For a while, our own player, Andy Clarkson conducted, and I recall, he was a popular conductor before a new permanent Musical Director was found. Tony Moon was a trombonist from Cornwall. Tony decided it was time that the band started to enter competitions again. I can recall we entered an 'Own Choice Contest' held in Barnstaple. We played a March, a Hymn and Vaughan Williams English Folk Songs Suite, a piece that is still popular with band competitions today. Unfortunately, we did not win, but neither did we come last. This illustrated to the 'Brass Band' community that once again, Tavistock had an up-and-coming band and was worthy of taking part in competitions.

Andy Myers conducts the band at a performance in Tavistock Bandstand c. 1978 note the sign board, in front of the band, which shows details from the Town's Crest. It can, also, be seen in much earlier pictures where, again, it was proudly displayed in front of the band.

**A Chilly Concert in Tavistock Bandstand - March 1980.
I can be seen top left next to the horn player.**

I recall that these years were happy times with the band. It was a happy relief from schoolwork and working on my parent's dairy farm. Being brought up with three brothers, we were all expected to do our bit of manual labour. I helped in the milking parlour and was responsible for retrieving the herd of cows from a far-off grass pastures. This was not much fun when the rain was pouring down, which it often did in Tavistock. The farm was large and even just this task involved a walk of a couple of miles. This continued before and after school as a child, so the chance to escape and play in the band with other kids was, to say the least, more than welcome.

My neighbour, Steve Page, [front middle in previous picture] gave me a lift to and from the band for many years. Together with his wife Jenny and their two daughters they were, I suppose, at this time quite the weekend's surrogate family. We would pack our lunches into Tupperware plastic boxes and travel off with the band to fetes and those lovely sunny summer days on Looe seafront. My favourite sandwich was cheese and sliced raw onion. These often became quite potent after a few hours in a warm plastic box! But a very tasty snack, sat on the beach at Looe seafront waiting for the allocated time for the band to play. Everyone would laugh, and pretend to run away, but this didn't bother me, I was used to being on my own.

It might sound a little sad, but my parents rarely came to listen to me play in the band. My Mother did a few times years later at the concerts in the town hall. But I don't think my Father ever came or heard me play. But I did have many happy days with the Page family. Steve was a real brass band enthusiast, and hoped, one day, to master his chosen instrument, the trombone. Unfortunately, he passed away several years ago before achieving his goal. I can still hear his favourite phrase of exasperation "Gordon Bennett!"

.

Chapter 5 – Happy Banding 1980 – 1990

"Some days you get up and put the horn to your chops and it sounds pretty good and you win. Some days you try and nothing works and the horn wins. This goes on and on and then you die and the horn wins." –
Dizzy Gillespie - *Jazz Trumpeter*

In 1981, the Band Committee decided it would be a good idea to honour one of its previous Musical Directors by presenting a memorial trophy at the band's Annual November Town Hall Concert. So, in November 1981, Michelle Davey became the first recipient of the David Carthew Memorial Trophy. It was awarded to the young member who had shown improvement and promise during the previous year. This was to become a trophy that was much sought after by the younger members of the band. I was lucky enough to win it a few years later in 1983.

Most improved player Claire Hutchison receives the David Carthew Memorial Trophy in 1987.

Later in 1981, after a further Contest in Paignton, Tony Moon left as Musical Director and for a while, the band was taken by Rod Short, the band's soprano cornet player. The band kept a good nucleus of members/players with a full tuba, trombone, horn and cornet section. We always seemed to have a great 'turnout' each year; in July, for the Tavistock Carnival, although, looking back, I think we might have had a few players from other local bands to boost our own numbers.

1981 - Competition at the Festival Theatre Paignton. Note our newly acquired green uniforms and Conductor Tony Moon with his best brown suit and orange shirt and tie. It reminds me just how close to the 70's we were in 1981.

During a particularly well-attended autumn concert around this time, it was decided to form a fund-raising and supporters' group. It was given the name, the Tavistock Town Band Association and, for many years, the founder and Secretary was Heather Campbell. Heather, together with her band of helpers, held numerous 'bring and buy' sales, stalls and other fund-raising events. Then as today, running a brass band was an expensive business, with each member being provided with an instrument, a uniform and music to play, along with other essential equipment like music stands and instrument mutes. We were lucky to have support from the Town Council who gave us our band rehearsal premises at a 'pepper corn' rent. That civic pride, we spoke about, was alive and well in the West Country town of Tavistock.

Young players Michelle Davey, Peter Goater and Joanne Davey.

The fundraising association ran for many years, providing the band with a steady means of income in addition to fees received for playing at engagements. Unfortunately, Heather moved away from the area, and when no volunteers were forthcoming to coordinate fund-raising events the association dis-banded. Throughout the passing years, the band tried to encourage the parents of children in the band and local people generally to support the band by forming another fund-raising group, but as today, people had busy lives. Apart from having their children play in the band parents seemed not to want to be any more involved, and so the band was left reliant on income from paid gigs and donations alone.

The band's next full-time Musical Director was L.G. Davies, who was known as 'Algy', yet another trombonist and peripatetic music teacher from Saltash. He was quite a laid-back character and would often turn up a little late to practices still puffing away at his continual string of cigarettes. He adopted a teacher's approach to learning music and so the band's musical ability rapidly improved. His plan of action was for the band to concentrate on playing entertaining concerts rather than spending loads of time learning one piece of music to play at a competition, and the players in the band at the time welcomed the idea, and a vast amount of new music was purchased to make this happen. To appear smart, for our new type of concerts, the band purchased a new set of uniforms, this time in blue. Unfortunately, 'Algy's' commitments were many and so he left only to make way for yet another trombonist to take on the baton. What was it with trombonists and their desire to hold a baton in preference to a trombone?

It appears I'm the only person 'in step' – Tavistock Square early 1980s.

A fine set of tubas / basses leading the band at Tavistock Carnival.

Tavistock's annual Carnival is organised by the Lions Club and held on the second Saturday in July raising money for local charities. Don't be deceived by the apparent sunshine, shown in this picture, as some years the rain would be running down the inside of your leg. I'm only glad I played the cornet rather than one of those rain collecting tubas.

Here I am, with Michelle Davey, in 1981 with our new green uniforms.

Here I am, compering our 'Last Night of the Proms' concerts at Sterts Theatre, Upton Cross, Bodmin. 2009 – 2015

"We had some great fun!"

BATON CHARGE ... Algy Davies, new conductor of Tavistock Town Band.

Band leader promises 'totally different' sound

TAVISTOCK's new bandmaster is Lloyd 'Algy' Davies, 45, who is a peripatetic brass teacher for North and East Cornwall and has been a professional musician since he was 15.

He lives in Saltash with his music - teacher wife, Elaine, and their four musical children, aged from six to 13.

His main instrument is the trombone, which he studied under the principal trombonist of the BBC Symphony Orchestra, but he also plays every other brass instrument, double bass and cello.

After many years as a professional jazzman and session musician he came to the West Country, where he had hoped to more or less retire from dashing round the world playing jazz.

'But,' he says, 'then I met up with Rod Mason.' And when Don Lusher was in Plymouth recently, they shared a stage for half an hour.

Now he spends a lot of time organising youth orchestras.

He plans to make Tavistock Town Band more of a concert band. 'Many town bands seem to concentrate on winning contests,' he said. 'But I think if they give good concerts they can win the contests anyway.'

'I've started working them hard and someone is always telling me they are absolutely exhausted after rehearsals.'

The band plans an autumn concert in the Town Hall, and Algy has already begun writing arrangements. He promises: 'It'll be totally different from everything people have heard before. There'll be a few surprises . . .'

But before the band can realise its full potential it needs a few key players. Algy is on the look-out for a couple of cornettists and a tenor horn player.

In a few years he might even be able to rustle them up from inside his own family. His children are beginning, he says, to have designs on brass instruments.

And they have plenty of choice. In his house is at least one of every instrument in the orchestra.

A newspaper cutting saved from the Tavistock Times Gazette.

L.G. (Algy) Davies holds the baton - Tavistock Bandstand.

The band is shown here, again at the bandstand in Tavistock Park and pleasure grounds. In the front [far right] are two staunch supporters Winnie and Joe. For many years they would come along and hold a collecting tin while we played. They must have helped collect substantial amounts over the years as they were certainly not 'backwards in coming forward' and would be more than happy to approach people who had stopped to enjoy the music. Winnie even wore one of the old band's green uniform jackets and made herself an official 'Band Collector' armband. Three of Algy's four children also joined the band and are seen standing in the front of this picture. I can be seen standing to the left of Algy, the conductor.

Following Algy's departure, due to other music project pressures, yet another trombonist joined us as Musical Director. Mike Kempster was a young teacher at Callington School and, therefore, he immediately had a great rapport with the younger members of the band. Mike's popularity and choice of new music took the band to an even greater standard, and we entered the South West Brass Band Association Regional Contest in Bristol and were pleased with the result, achieving a creditable 14th place out of 29 Bands. This was indeed some achievement. On this occasion we all agreed the man in the box was not 'all bad', after all.

BAND NEW ..., Tavistock band members pictured with their newly appointed conductor, Mike Kempster from Callington.

Following much organisation and effort by Tony Turland; in September 1986 the band made its first trip to Tavistock's twin town of Pontivy in Brittany, France. Tony had been elected band Chairman in January 1982 following the resignation of Andy Clark, who had held the position for many years. Tony worked tirelessly to organise the twinning events and he had a long and important relationship with the band and held the position of Chairman until February 1997, when work, health and other personal commitments led him not to apply for re-election. The band travelled to France every other year and made connections with our French counterparts the 'Orchestra Harmonie de Pontivy' and they also made trips to Tavistock on many occasions. Often, while travelling to France on the Brittany ferry from Plymouth to the French port of Roscoff, we would play a concert on the boat. This was usually a night-time crossing and often the smell of engine oil combined with the potential for rough seas meant that not everyone who started the piece of music would be around to hear the final chord.

**Conductor Mike Kempster sat in the middle (front row)
I'm under the arrow at the back.**

When Mike Kempster left, to take a new teaching post away from the area, the band again found itself without a conductor. For a while, the baton was shared between Greg Woods and Brian Fisher, both of whom were competent tuba players within the Band.

At this time local Councillor Gordon Foden was a great supporter of the band, and as the owner of a small pub on Plymouth Road, The Virtuous Lady, members would often find themselves there after band practice. The band often performed a concert squeezed onto his small terrace. The site was eventually sold to McDonald's, but this only lasted a few years, due to the lack of support from locals, and it soon closed to become a Lidl's supermarket.

In this picture we can see Greg Woods conducting the band at 'The Virtuous Lady' Public House, Plymouth Road, Tavistock, now the site of Lidl's Supermarket.

Band supporter Brian Foden [white jumper] looks on, in the background. Our next conductor, Ian Whitburn can be seen to the left of the arrow. Surprise surprise! - he was yet another trombonist.

In 1988, connections were made with a new band formed in Plymouth, called Plymouth Brass. Its Musical Director, Ian Whitburn, agreed to also conduct Tavistock for a while to help out. As time went on, it became clear that each band could not exist without the other due to the shortage of players, and the decision was made to amalgamate the two bands. It was also decided to amalgamate the two band names with the new band being called Tavistock Brass. Looking to promote a more modern image, it was felt that this name would help as it was snappy and descriptive. Soon no Plymouth Brass players remained, and it became clear the entire Plymouth Band had been absorbed, and yet another Brass Band had vanished almost without trace.

Larger-than-life character Brian Fisher conducts a concert at the Tavistock Town Hall. Front left are brother and sister, Penny & Duncan Newman. They were to return to the band in 2015 with Duncan as Musical Director.

Our printed programmes were typed on a manual typewriter, with a hand drawn cover. You must remember this was the 1980s.

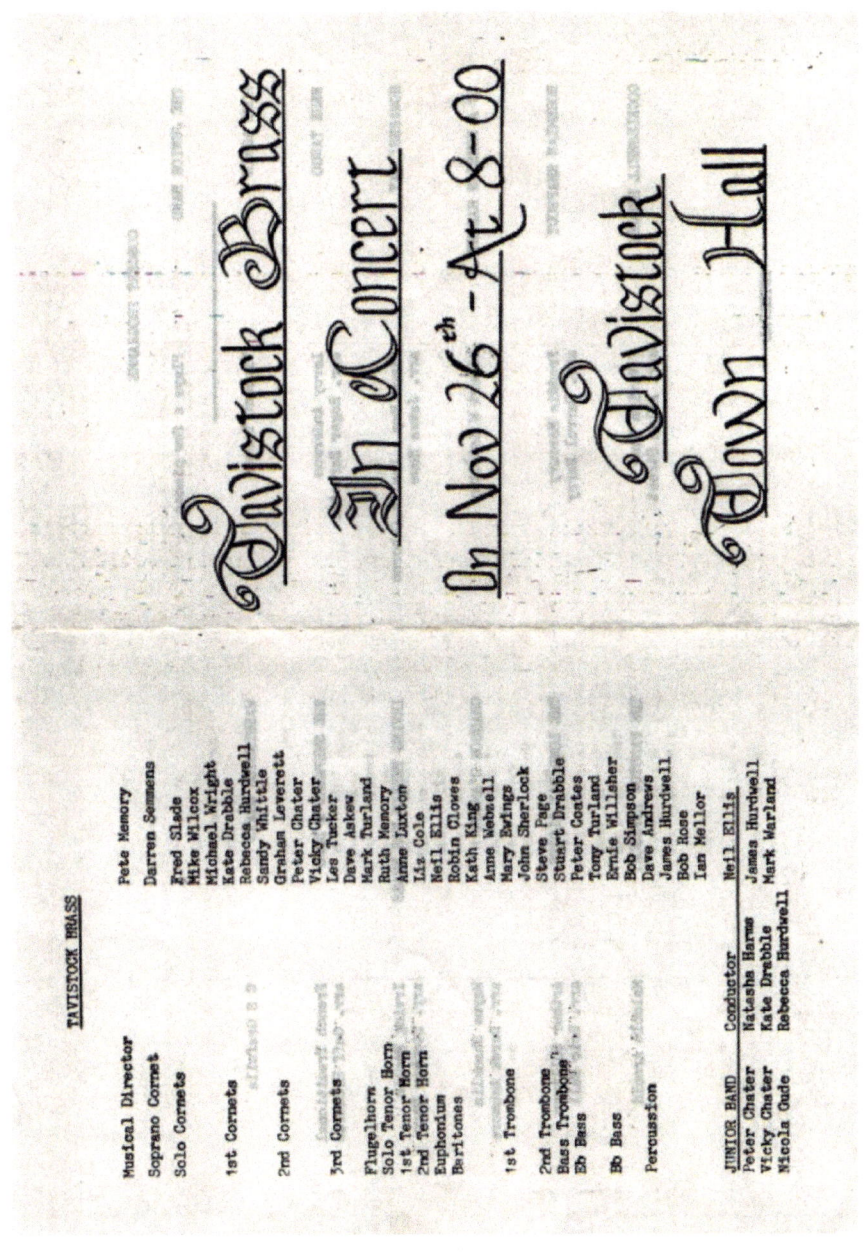

A typical concert programme from the late 1980s.

Here, our programme, included 'The Padstow Lifeboat' a piece still hugely popular in brass band concerts today.

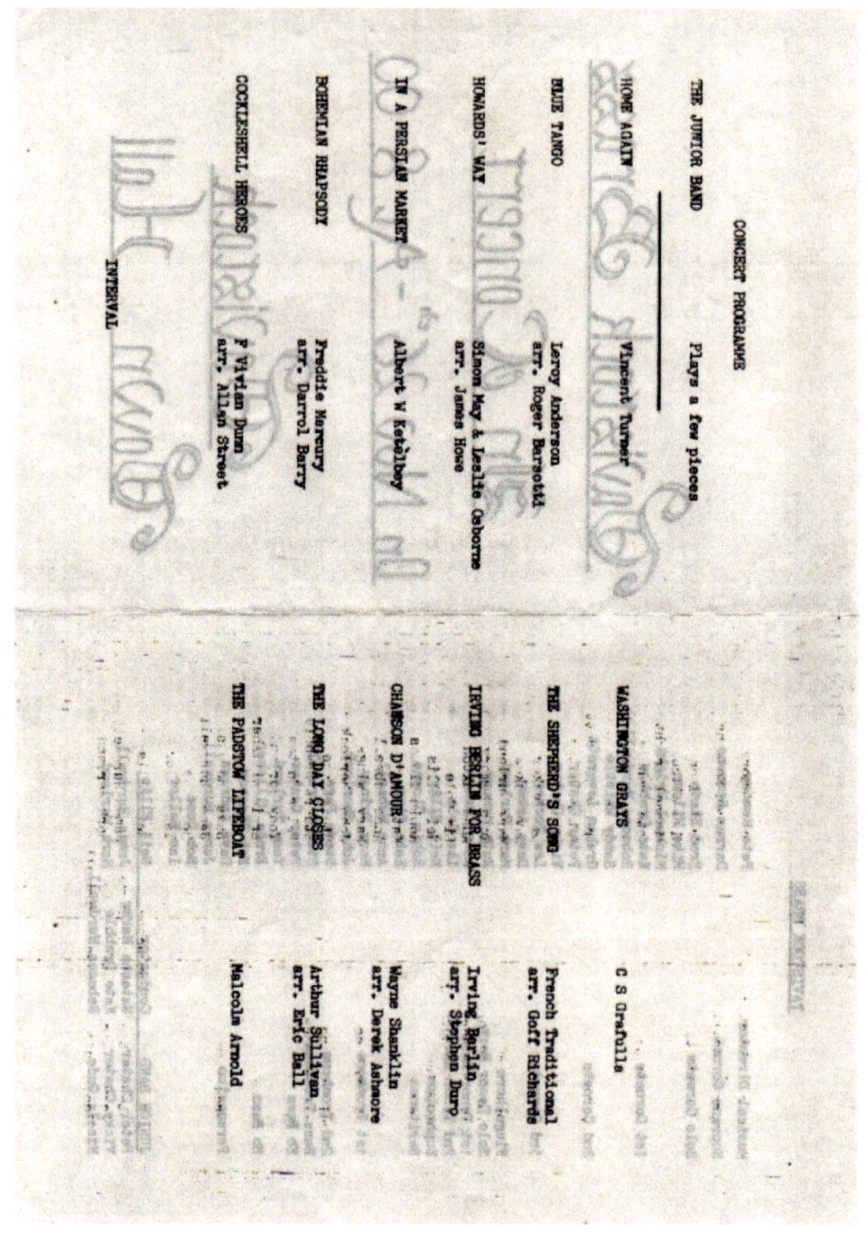

Just about every band, at this time, played the 'Howard's Way' theme.

We entered the South West Brass Band competition in Bristol. The fourth section test piece was Drake Rimmer's test piece 'Othello'. St Gennys band, from North Cornwall, took first place. It's not recorded how many bands played or what position we came, but normally, around this time at least fifteen to twenty bands would take part in the fourth section. From the smiles, on our faces, we either did quite well or perhaps this photo was taken before we played. At least it was another day out representing the town of Tavistock.

In this picture, we can see the band at the South West Brass Band Association's Championships held at the Festival Theatre in Paignton on the 5th of November 1988.

The Town of Tavistock's Coat of Arms

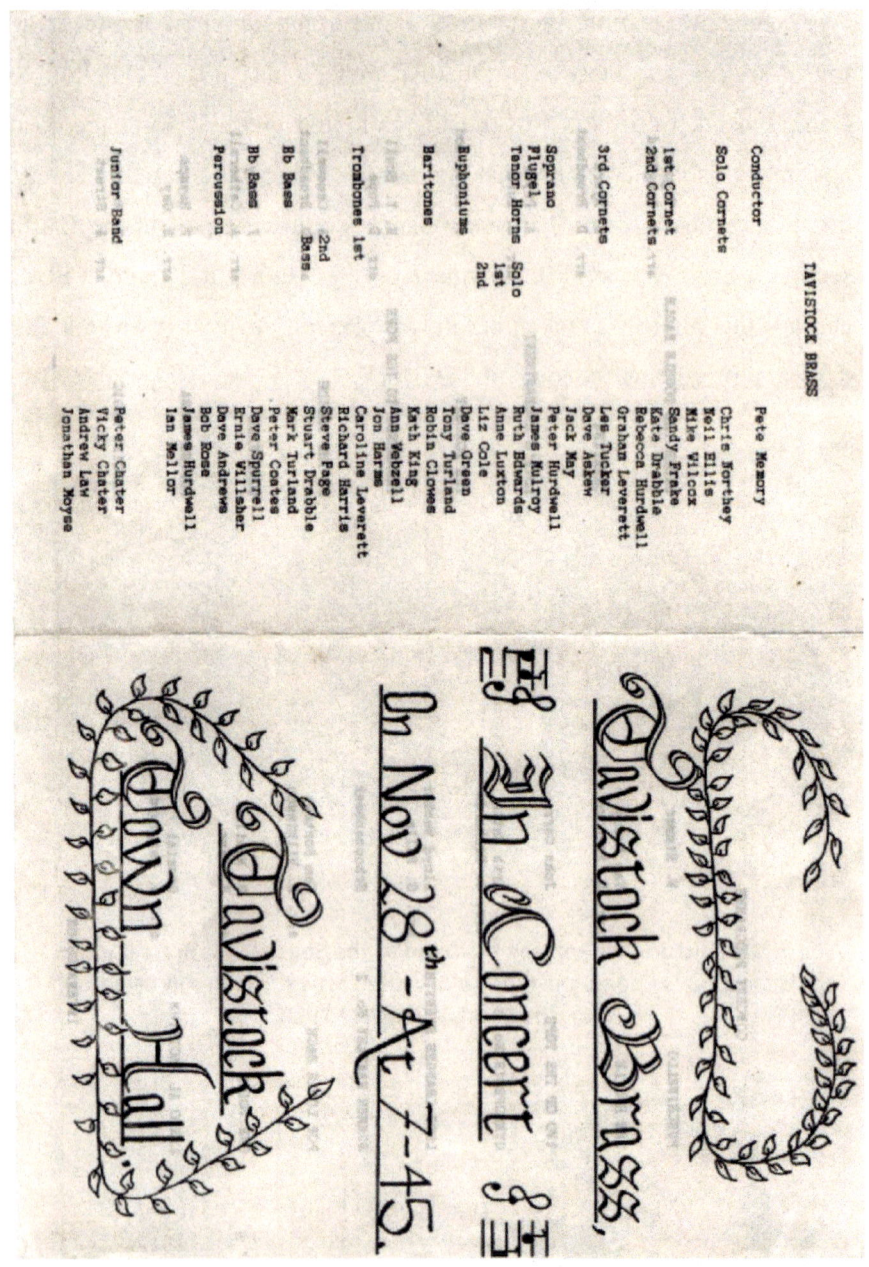

Our annual Tavistock Town Hall concert was always held in November, and this continued until we moved to September to align with the BBC Proms last night concert on the TV.

'Pop Looks Bach' was the popular theme to the TV programme, 'Sky Sunday'. Not an easy piece to play, but evidentially, we managed it.

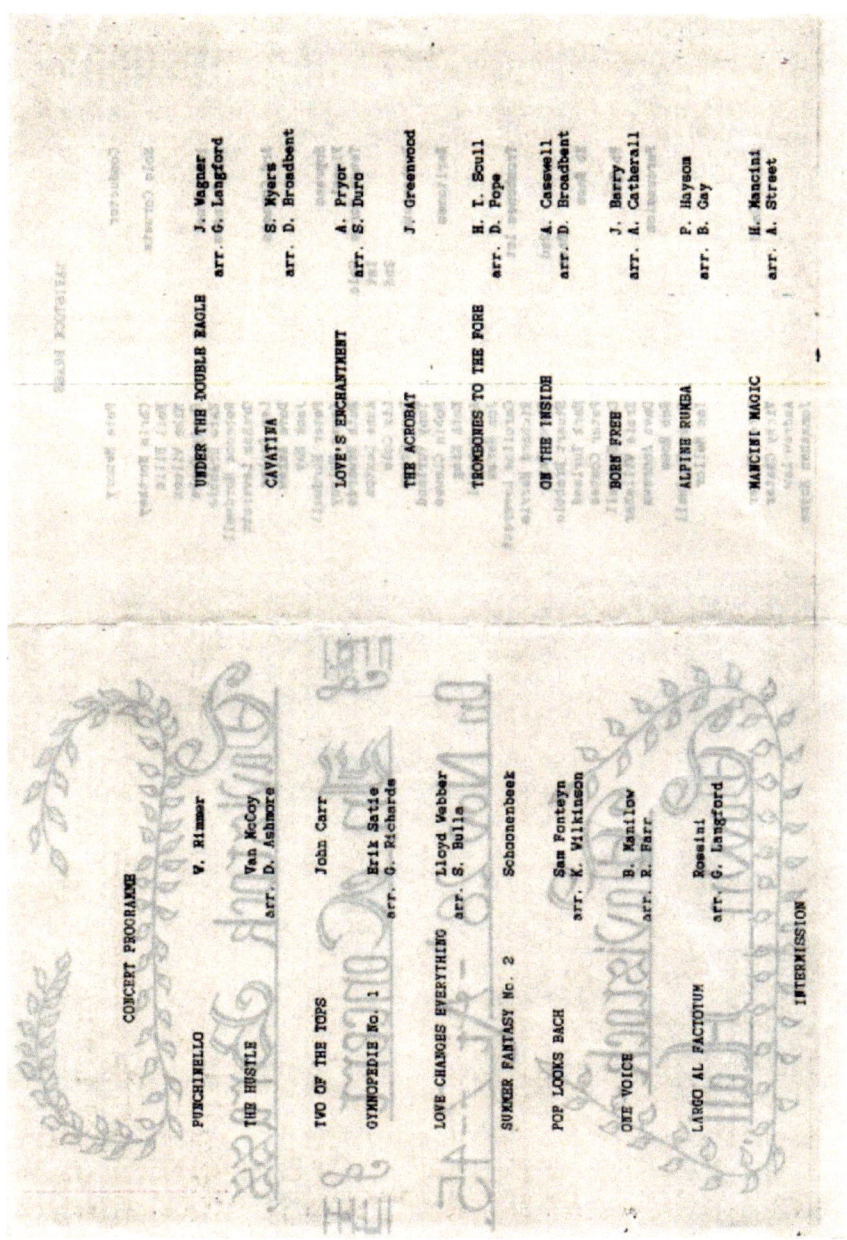

CONCERT PROGRAMME

PUNCHINELLO	V. Rimmer	
THE HUSTLE	Van McCoy	arr. D. Ashmore
TWO OF THE TOPS	John Carr	
GYMNOPEDIE No. 1	Erik Satie	arr. G. Richards
LOVE CHANGES EVERYTHING	Lloyd Webber	arr. S. Bulla
SUMMER FANTASY No. 2	Schoonenbeek	
POP LOOKS BACH	Sam Fonteyn	arr. K. Wilkinson
ONE VOICE	B. Manilow	arr. R. Farr
LARGO AL FACTOTUM	Rossini	arr. G. Langford

INTERMISSION

UNDER THE DOUBLE EAGLE	J. Wagner	arr. G. Langford
CAVATINA	S. Myers	arr. D. Broadbent
LOVE'S ENCHANTMENT	A. Pryor	arr. S. Duro
THE ACROBAT	J. Greenwood	
TROMBONES TO THE FORE	H. T. Scull	arr. D. Pope
ON THE INSIDE	A. Casewell	arr. D. Broadbent
BORN FREE	J. Barry	arr. A. Catherall
ALPINE RUMBA	P. Hayson	arr. B. Gay
MANCINI MAGIC	H. Mancini	arr. A. Street

South West Brass Band Contest at the Festival Theatre Paignton 1990.

H.R.H. Prince Edward drops in to listen to our Concert at Tavistock Bandstand in 1988.

Christmas carolling at the Queen's Head St Anne's Chapel c. 1987.

A Village Hall Christmas Concert with members joining the HMP Prison band.

A pre-concert talk by Musical Director, Ian Whitburn, before going on stage at Tavistock Town Hall.

A fund-raising concert in Tavistock Pannier Market.

Chapter 6 – Tavistock Carnival

"Brass bands are all very well in their place – outdoors and several miles away." – **Sir Thomas Beecham** - *Conductor*

Tavistock Carnival is held on the second Saturday in July. It starts where Down Road meets Whitchurch Road, by the cattle market, next to the Market Inn and its infamous cobbled floor stable that used to be our rehearsal room many years before. The participating floats and walking entries would line up in Down Road, ready for judging, before we set off down Whitchurch Road and through the Town Square before turning left and heading down Plymouth Road towards the Sir Francis Drake statue. Plymouth Road is the long approach road to the town centre and it was always a welcome sight to see the statue as this marked almost the halfway point on the parade. I remember one year the band having to follow a horse and carriage – that was not a good year!

The Sir Francis Drake Statue, at the end of Plymouth Road, Tavistock.

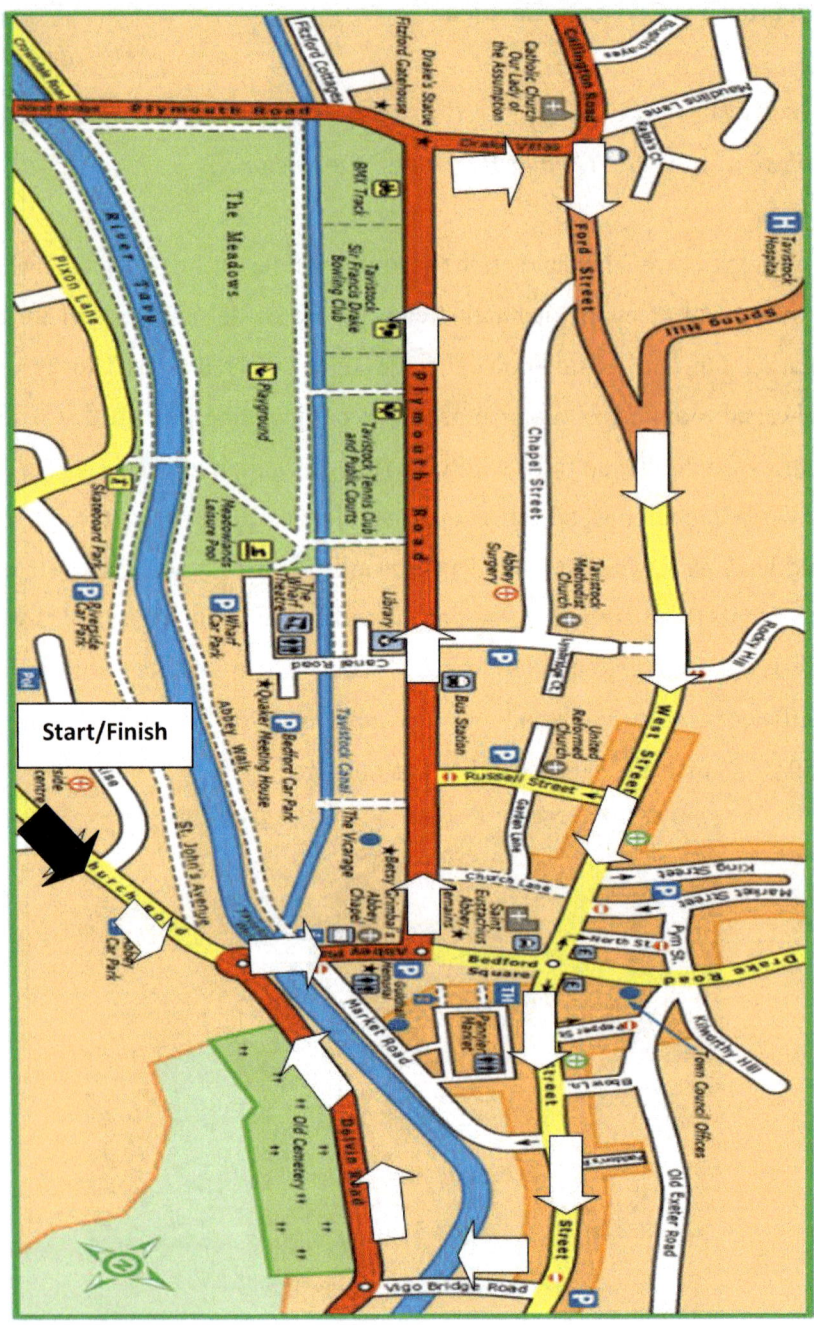

The carnival parade route took us all around the town, and back again.

The Sir Francis Drake statue had been erected by the Duke of Bedford in 1883 to commemorate the town's most famous Son, Sir Francis Drake. The solid bronze statue was cast by Sir Joseph Edgar Boehm. Drake was born at a farm in Crowndale Road, Tavistock in 1540, after which he went on to become a famous sea captain, explorer, privateer, slave trader, naval officer, and politician, but is perhaps, best known for his circumnavigation of the world in a single expedition, on the Golden Hind, between 1577 and 1580 and for his leadership in the defeat against the Spanish Armada in 1588. It is said that he was playing bowls on Plymouth Hoe when he received news that he should depart to meet the Spanish invasion flotilla. But, he decided to finish his game of bowls before his departure.

Mike Whitburn leads the band in Tavistock Carnival.

To honour his memory, the Bowls Club in Tavistock is called the Tavistock Sir Francis Drake Bowling Club, and both my parents were members for many years, following their retirement from farming. The club is to be found on the Plymouth Road, next to the canal, which runs along the side of the park [the Meadows].

After passing the statue, the carnival parade would turn right at the Duke of York pub into Ford Street and up the hill, before descending the hill onto West Street. This area, with large buildings on either side of the road, was an excellent place to play a loud march as we proceeded down the hill towards the town centre. We would pass the crowds still in Bedford Square, then proceed through the main shopping area of Duke Street and Brook Street, before turning right and crossing the river Tavy [from where the town gets its name] over Vigo Bridge. Once over the bridge the parade would turn right onto Dolvin Road and proceed back towards the town square and Whitchurch Road, where we started from.

The band leaves Tavistock Square and turns into Plymouth Road.

This reminds me of the fact that, in 1644 King Charles himself came to Tavistock and stayed in the house of the Glanville family in Pym Street. He stayed in the town for a whole week, and his son later visited in 1645. He immortalised the town by declaring in later years whenever anyone mentioned the weather, "if it is raining anywhere in my kingdom, it will be raining in Tavistock", and having lived previously in the town for 49 years, I can confirm it has some of the greenest gardens and lawns in the country.

The 'Orchestre Harmonie de Pontivy' at the Bandstand in the Park.

The band hosted the first visit from our French counterparts, The 'Orchestre Harmonie de Pontivy' in May 1989. Together with the support of the Tavistock Town Council, we did our best to match the hospitality that had been shown to us during our previous visits to France. Our visitors were taken on a trip to the local National Trust property, Cotehele House, in the Tamar Valley, and the day ended with an evening reception in a room previously used by the band as rehearsal premises, the function room at the then Ordulph Arms. [Previously the Rural District's Council Offices in Pym Street]. Later in the evening, the French were introduced to West Country square dancing complete with the 'Dartmoor Pixie Band'. I can remember that tremendous fun was had by all.

Graham Leverett [cornet] and his daughter Caroline [cornet/ trombone] were tremendous assets to the band for many years.

The band regularly held fundraising events to pay for the cost of running the group. These included sponsored events, raffles, concerts and hand collections while playing in the park. Our main annual fundraising effort was playing Christmas carols in December, with the door-to-door street collections abandoned in the early 1980s in favour of playing in the town centre all day on Saturdays, throughout December. For many brass bands, the December Carolling season is an important fundraiser to see the band financially through the next year. At this time money collected went to the band and I cannot recall any amount being given to charity. While some people did own their instrument, most were provided, free of charge, to players by the band. The ongoing cost of new uniforms, replacing older instruments and rent meant finances were always on the agenda. In the mid 1980s and, perhaps, because I worked in a bank, I became the band's Treasurer, a post that I continued in until 2015.

Here we can see Ian Whitburn conducting the band at a village fete. Note the plethora of trombones, a popular instrument indeed, and the chosen instrument for many of our conductors over the years. This was certainly, a very happy time, in the band, with a full complement of players. It appears, I was not required on solo cornet, and can be seen in the 'back row', on soprano cornet.

The Band's sponsored 'Play a Concert' at Tavistock Pannier Market.

The band plays in France, in the town square in Pontivy, with the Trombone section playing their favourite Trio feature 'The Bold Gendarmes' [very apt given the location].

Another carnival parade – James Hurdwell on side drum and Tom Hurdwell playing marching cymbals, and also Tavistock Town Crier, Bob Rose on bass drum.

I can recall that, during this period, the band played at a great many parades and carnivals, and these included;

Tavistock
Mary Tavy
South Brent
Looe
Okehampton
Ashburton
Bovey Tracey
Lustleigh
Landulph
Ipplepen

[you might need to 'Google' that last location]

Like many times before, our musical director, Ian Whitburn, moved away from the area to take an employment opportunity elsewhere in the country, but it was not long before, yet another trombonist was appointed as Musical Director, Peter Memory, a Prison Officer at the nearby Dartmoor Prison. Like many of our musical directors around this time, Peter also preferred a lighter, popular music programme, and so the band continued its happy phase into the 1990s.

HMP Prison Dartmoor.

HMP Prison Dartmoor is only a few miles from Tavistock which lies on the edge of Dartmoor National Park. Many members of the band worked there over the years. In fact, so many members worked there that at one time we formed an HMP Brass Band and used to travel to Newbold Revel near Coventry to play at the passing out parades of the newly trained prison officers.

Here we can be seen on a trip to Coventry, to play in the HMP Band. Left to right – Ruth Memory, Anne Luxton, Liz Cole, Ann Webzell, Chris Northey-Youngs, Graham Leverett and Pete Memory. I can recall we all played very well, and luckily we didn't get "banged up!"

**In 1990 long standing member Les' Tucker married Rose,
Seen here with a trombone guard of honour.**

Another Pontivy trip - another parade. Our marching skills were well honed.

Yet another parade, this time, perhaps in Princetown? Here I am, in my trusty shades and in my usual marching position playing cornet behind Ruth on tenor horn.

Chapter 7 – Entente Cordiale

"Long live the difference, but long live the Entente Cordiale." – **Queen Elizabeth II**

After a further trip to the French twin town Pontivy in 1991, the band also travelled to Tavistock's other twin town, Celle in North Germany. The trip to Celle was a long one and involved a stop-over in Brussels. Once in Celle, the majority of the band stayed at a boarding school, which was empty due to school holidays. A good friend of mine, Ann Webzell, who played tenor horn in the band was fortunate to have friends who lived in Celle and so we were lucky enough to be able to enjoy full German home comforts.

Here we can see Peter Memory showing off his new white D.J. in our twin town of Celle, Germany. This was a full and happy band.

The main concert of the weekend was held at a large army barracks on the parade ground complete with a huge stage, lights, lasers and two enormous television screens which relayed the stage events to the watching crowds. It continued well into the evening and included many other bands and groups from other countries including Russia, France and Ireland. The whole event was a truly international event which must have taken considerable organisation and the audience numbered near to 20,000 people. The evening concluded with a spectacular laser show projected onto the huge main three-story buildings which surrounded the parade ground together with synchronised fireworks display and music.

The band worked hard to buy yet another set of new uniforms, this time with the colours harking back to the original black and red design. Like those early black and white photos from the band's archive, we too were all extremely proud to wear our new smart uniforms. In years to come, they would be stored in our music cupboard in the basement of the Council Chambers, before being thrown out sometime after 2015.

Our new Musical Director, Peter Memory's vision for the band was to promote the popularity of the band by introducing a lighter programme of music. Unfortunately, as had happened so many times in the past, Peter moved away due to a work promotion out of the area. The baton was then held, for a while, by an old friend of the band, Peter Coates. Peter had played in the band many times over the years and now brought his special style as Musical Director. Peter preferred what he called "jolly tunes" and our audiences really enjoyed his choice of music programme. Sadly, towards the end of 1992, Peter was forced to resign, due to ill health, and so the baton passed to yet another trombonist.

On parade in Pontivy, France, on one of our many 'Twinning Association' trips

Me on cornet behind Ruth Memory on tenor horn – another parade!

John Sherlock was a tall imposing person who, like Peter Memory and Peter Coates before him, worked for H.M. Prison Service. Luckily, John also favoured a lighter programme of music, although his 'manner' was not as light-hearted as Peter's had been, and this was something that was to cause problems a little later, having said that, it would have been difficult, for anyone to follow in the shoes of such a nice person as Peter Coates.

Peter Coates takes control.

The band made its 5th trip to France in September 1993 and then hosted a further French visit to Tavistock in May 1994. The band was proud to be asked to play at a special concert to celebrate visiting American Servicemen commemorating the town's involvement in the events of the

D-Day landings. The 29th US Infantry Division, commanded by Major General Charles H Gerhardt, was the first to arrive and set up camp in June 1943 on Whitchurch Down with its headquarters at Abbotsfield House [now Abbotsfield Hall Nursing Home]. In February 1944, the Supreme Allied Commander; General Dwight D Eisenhower – who became US President in 1953 – inspected H Company of the 29th Division in Bedford Square. Just before D Day, General Eisenhower and the Overall Land Forces Commander, Field Marshall Lord Montgomery, met at Abbotsfield House for a conference and a memorial plaque was mounted over the fireplace in honour of this visit. It is still there today.

1944 General Eisenhower visits the American troops based in Tavistock.

The concert was held at Tavistock Comprehensive School, in the main hall. This was to be John Sherlock's last band engagement as shortly after, a special meeting was held to sort out various discord and friction within the Band. Brass Bands seem to suffer badly from politics and sometimes controlling individuals wield the power to decide between having a happy band or a disgruntled one. Unfortunately, sometimes committees seem happy to cut off their noses to spite their face and so under committee pressure John resigned, and once again, the band was left without a Musical Director.

Abbotsfield Hall as it is today.

The Committee met to discuss the way forward and, after no new conductor came forward, they decided that it would be unwise to appoint the leader of the Training Band to the position of 'main band' Musical Director due to his young age and inexperience. It was this decision that led to further unrest within the band which culminated in the Training Band leader and most of the competent trainees, together with a few of the main band members, walking out to form their own band, Stannary

Brass. However, this still left a dedicated, strong and enthusiastic nucleus of able musicians who were now tasked with taking the band forward to, yet another new chapter and it was not long before the band found its new Musical Director, John Quaye, an ex-Royal Marine Band Master. Under the older experienced hand of John, the band soon went from strength to strength. As the standard and overall ability of the band improved, more competent players were attracted to join. Many of the new players travelled from Plymouth, Plympton and even Cornwall to attend band practice and engagements. The Training Band also began to grow under the strong direction and leadership of professionally trained musicians Chris and Ros Incledon. Chris had previously been a musician in the armed forces and Ros' was a very talented classically trained pianist. Both were really lovely people. Unfortunately, Chris passed away from Cancer, and in subsequent years all our collections from our Christmas collection period went to Cancer related charities in his memory.

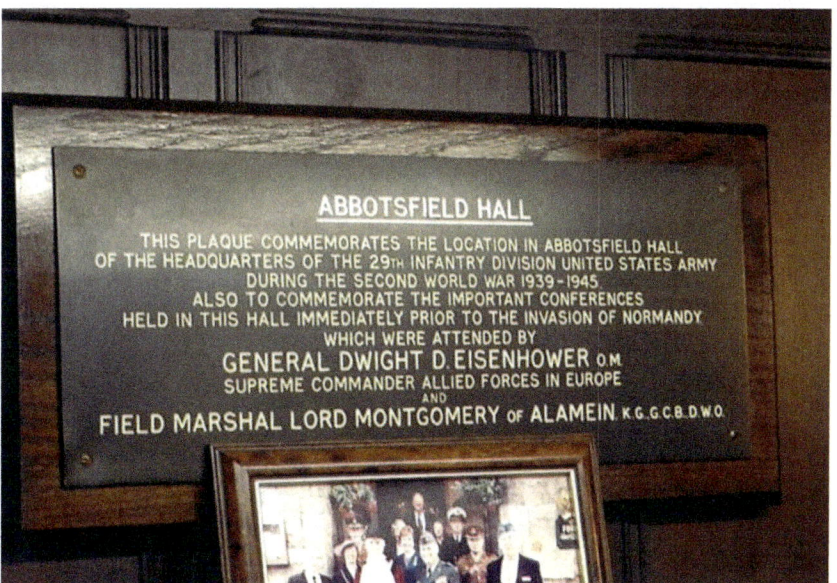

Concert programme for our 'Last Night of the Proms' concert at Sterts Theatre 2013

Please be upstanding for The National Anthem

Tavistock Versatile Brass Ensemble

Unsung Hero Fanfare	Matt Conway *	
Hometown Boy March	Karl L. King *	
If we Hold on Together	James Horner *	
Final Countdown	Joey Tempest*	

Sterts Singers

One Voice	Barry Manilow #	
Shine	Gary Barlow #	
Miss Saigon selection	Schonberg/Boublil	
Something Inside So Strong	Labi Siffre	

Bodmin Town Band

Florentine March	Julius Fucik	
Singing In The Rain	Nacio Herb Brown	
Such Love	Paul Drury	
Lord Of The Dance	Ronan Hardiman	

Tavistock Versatile Brass Ensemble

O Fortuna	Carl Orff *	
A Kind & Gentle Soul	James Swearingen *	
Into the Storm	Robert W. Smith *	
Pirates of the Caribbean	Hans Zimmer *	

Sterts Singers

Easter Hymn from Cavalleria Rusticana soloist Kate Walker	Pietro Mascagni	
I Will Follow Him Soloist Lydia Edge	Pourcel/Maurie #	

Bodmin Town Band

The Impresario	Domenico Cimarosa	
Gabriel's Oboe	Ennio Morriconi	
Breezin' Down Broadway	Goff Richards	

Finale

Pomp & Circumstance March No.1 in D (Land of Hope & Glory)	Edward Elgar	
Fantasia on British Sea Songs	Henry Wood	
Rule Britannia (Soloist – Kate Walker)	Thomas Arne*	
Jerusalem	Hubert Parry	

A programme for one of our later 'Last Night of the Proms' style concerts.

Chapter 8 – Centenary Celebrations

"One good thing about music, when it hits you, you feel no pain." – **Bob Marley** – *Musician*

The band enjoyed its sixth and finest trip yet to twin town Pontivy in September 1995. John retired from the band in 1996 and our new conductor was yet another trombonist, Dr Tony Evans. Tony, a professional musician, ex-Welsh Guardsman and proprietor of two local music shops, Mainly Music and Maestro's Music Shops, had helped the band many times in past years but had not wished to take the baton due to the commitment required. But now Tavistock had the makings of a band of ability, and Tony was keen to set out his plans to continue the improvement within the band.

Me playing a cornet solo 'My Love is Like a Red Red Rose' at the Moorland Links Hotel, Roborough Down in 1997 with Tony Evans conducting.

Tony was a firm believer that taking part in competitions was a major way of determining standard and ability and so in September 1996, the band entered Penzance Contest competition in the depths of Cornwall. This was the band's first contest in many years and, after undertaking intensive rehearsals, we knew we had a good chance of doing well. The band played excellently, and people jumped as we started a march called 'The Cossack' and they rustled through their programmes to see which band was playing such a difficult march so well. The adjudicator placed us in fourth position and only four points behind the band which came first. Many of the people who had heard us play were surprised at the result as they really thought we should have gained first place. Never mind, this was our best contest result for many years, and we had shown the longstanding bands of Cornwall that, perhaps, they would have to look out for us in the future.

For the centenary concert I played solo cornet. Here's my best 'bib & tucker'.

After taking the band for almost a year, Tony was so pleased with the progress and commitment within the band that he offered for his business, Maestro's Music, to sponsor the band, an offer that the band was pleased to accept as it brought substantial financial benefits. However, it did entail yet another variation on the band name to Tavistock Town Band (Maestro's Music).

Tavistock Town Hall with its Victorian vaulted ceiling, and at one end above a fireplace a Minstrel's Gallery.

One of my early 'MicroSoft Publisher' programme designs for our popular 'Last Night of the Proms' concerts.

Tavistock Town Hall is adorned with original oil paintings of the town's great and good of yester-year.

1997 saw the band celebrate its centenary year with a concert at Tavistock Town Hall. We tried to invite as many of the band's previous players as we could find, and it felt great to get so many supporters of the band together. Tony organised a special programme of traditional brass band favourites. I remember playing solo cornet and the evening being a great success. Many other Town Hall concerts were held over the coming years and our themed concert of the "Last Night of the Proms" was always the most popular, so much so that it has now been copied by almost every brass band in the land. I cannot claim that we were the first brass band to adopt this theme, but I think we were the first one in our locality.

Tony Evans M.D.1996 - 2001

Army Of The Nile (March)	Alford	
Plymouth Hoe (Overture)	Ansell	
Bedford Square (Written To Commemorate the Refurbishment Of Tavistock's Square)	S P Williams	
Crown Imperial (Coronation March)	Walton	
Presentations Of Annual Band Awards		
Easter Hymn (Choir Item)	Mascagni	**Cantique De Jean Racine** — Fauré
Linden Lea (Choir Item)	Vaughan Williams	**Real Slow Drag** — Scott Joplin
The Last Rose Of Summer (Soprano Soloist - Elaine Rockell)	T Moore	**Rule Britannia** — Arne
How Great Thou Art (Cornet Soloist - Steve Williams)	Traditional	**Fantasy On British Sea Songs** — Arr. Langford
Prince Eugenes March (Processional)	J Clarke Arr. T Evans	**Pomp & Circumstance March No.1** — Elgar
		Hallelujah Chorus — Handel
		Jerusalem — Parry
Chorus Of The Hebrew Slaves	Verdi	**A Gaelic Blessing** — Rutter
		National Anthem

Interval Of 20 Minutes

The Raffle Will Be Drawn During The Interval
Please Check Your Tickets Against The Prizes On Your Way Out

A Programme to one of our early 'Last Night of the Proms' concerts

Chapter 9 – Bugle Contest

"Being underestimated is one of the biggest competitive advantages you can have. Embrace it." – **Unknown**

Bugle is a village in mid-Cornwall, in the parish of Treverbyn, and is to be found about five miles north of St Austell. In 1912 a group of villagers founded the West of England Bandsmen's Festival. It's very likely that they only expected the event to last for a couple of years, and to think here we are over a hundred years later. Their plan was to raise funds for a new working men's institute and a new band room for the village brass band. Each original committee member deposited a gold sovereign as a guarantee of a prize fund totalling at least £45.

The home of the judge is seen here, the white tent in front of the performance Platform. [West of England Bandsmen's Festival archive]

The first competition was held on the 14th of September 1912 and had eleven bands enter, including one from Tiverton in Devon. The day's events were reported in the Bodmin Guardian, describing the day as a great success; "There have been other band contests in Cornwall before Saturday but the important festival which took place at Bugle was by a long way the most ambitious and triumphantly successful the Delectable Duchy has known".

To start with entries to the competition were limited to only bands from the West of England, but, in 1926, this restriction was removed and after that any band could enter. Also, in that year a deportment class was introduced, and since the adjudicators were usually military people they were, no doubt, keen to watch for appearance and precision as the bands marched pass them through the village on their way to the contest field.

The competition held in the following year was known as the Royal Trophy Contest, as it was granted royal patronage with the presentation, by the Prince of Wales, of a magnificent silver trophy. However, until 1934 there was a restriction that only a West Country band was allowed to win this particular prize. For many years, any band who won the trophy three years in a row would also receive individual medals for the members of the band, with the members of St Dennis band being the first to achieve this in 1922. They went on to, also, achieve this feat on six other occasions. The other bands to also achieve this were Camborne, on five occasions and St Austell once. Other Cornish bands to win the Royal Trophy in consecutive years include Bodmin, Falmouth, Mount Charles and Redruth.

After 1934, when the rule changed to allow non-Cornish bands being able to take the Royal Trophy back across the Tamar, it has been won by Munn and Feltons [now Virtuosi GUS Footwear], Black Dyke, Morris Motors, and Melingriffith.

The contest continued each year until 1933 when it was cancelled due to financial problems. Bad weather during the previous two years led to a poor uptake in participating bands, and the committee decided that it would be unwise to go ahead. The two world wars, and more recently the COVID-19 pandemic also saw the contest being cancelled.

The streets lined with spectators, as a band marches through the village. [West of England Bandsmen's Festival archive]

The draw for bands to attend the small clay-mining village of Bugle is amazing. At the outset, back in 1912, the draw of a hefty monetary prize was, I'm sure, a big draw, but nowadays, the main draw is the sheer fun of a good day's brass banding. The whole village is transformed into a festival location, with each band making their own choice of which march to play for the deportment prize. Each band marches to the performance site starting at a point near the village pub, the Bugle Inn. The pavements, on either side of the road, are packed with people. Bugle really is a most strange location for such a day's events. The large slag clay heaps form huge mountains which surround the village, they are so large that they can be seen for miles. In the past before C.G.I. they were popular locations for filming TV programmes, and have appeared in a number of episodes of Dr Who and Blake's Seven.

The contest has been held at two locations within the village. From 1912 until 1966 it was the beautiful grounds of Penial House. But, as the event outgrew that location, a decision was made to move to Molinnis Park, the home of Bugle Football Club. The move was made with some regret, as some wrote; "We missed the beautiful setting of Penial; it had been a wonderful venue and had become synonymous with the event, but with poor parking and a lack of facilities it made it no longer tenable". I imagine with the regular downpours of rain it was almost impossible to get cars out of the parking fields which were on a slope.

Before the start of each competition there is the ritual of locking away the adjudicator into a small fabric tent which sits in front of the raised stage on which the competing bands play. Only then is the draw made to decide in which order the bands will play. The idea being, the 'man in the box' as he is referred to has no idea which band is playing, and just has to listen. There are various classes for both senior and youth bands, and a recent addition of a training band section.

Spectators listen to the band at Bugle Contest early 20th century.
[West of England Bandsmen's Festival archive]

Each band is given a number, and after reporting to the contest official for 'registration' [more of that later], the band is allowed to proceed up the steps to the raised platform and ready themselves for their performance, placing their trusty clothes pegs to secure their paper music to the music stands. The adjudicator blows a whistle to indicate he is ready for the performance to begin. Originally, the bands had to perform their renditions standing, and it was not until the mid 1930's that chairs and seating was introduced. The stage at the original Penial site was a little strange as it was mounted on top of a hedge, with the performers entering from one field and leaving the stage into another.

In most cases the bands in each section, all play the same piece of music to enable the adjudicator to make a fair judgment between the bands. Originally, these pieces would have been transcriptions of known classical or orchestral pieces, but in later years, test pieces were especially written for the brass band genre. In 1912 the main test pieces was 'Maritana', a favourite at many early contests.

The festival is certainly a famous Cornish brass banding tradition where old friends meet and chat over a pasty and a cup of tea. People sit and listen in their deck chairs or wander around and chat with folk they last saw 12 months ago. They listen for the mistakes of the opposing bands and hope that the adjudicator also heard that little 'slip up', after all, often it is these little things which can make all the difference. Despite the carnival atmosphere, the whole event is seen by many as a most serious musical event of the year, and as one supporter put it "never mind the Nationals, who won at Bugle?"

But what if it rains? You might ask, well the short answer is you get wet. Many an outside Cornish event has been dogged by bad weather. In an effort to try and avoid this, the whole event was moved from September to August, and then in 1951 to June, as we all know it never rains in June! In 1971 heavy rain and gale force winds were forecast, and a Marquee was erected and for the first time the contest was held undercover. As it happened the day remained dry, but the following year a canopy was erected over the stage area and now each year, at least while each competing band is playing, they are at least shielded from potential rain. However, the wind can still present a problem, hence the need for a sturdy supply of clothes pegs.

**Cars have to park tightly in the field – 1951.
[West of England Bandsmen's Festival archive]**

The cost of putting on such an event is considerable, and the organising committee is, therefore, thankful not only to the bands paying an entrance fee, but also to the paying supporters for their entrance fee to the football ground where the stage is erected. The event has also gained sponsorship from IMERYS, the giant china clay company, and its predecessors ECLP and ECC, whose donations and financial support has been substantial, along with that of other local businesses.

With the amateur adjudicators in the audience comparing their notes and predictions, the day is brought to a close with a march back up through the village by the winning bands. In 1928, Charles Baker, conductor of

St Dennis Band wrote "I shall not quickly forget those closing scenes near the square. Every window was occupied, and every band got its full-hearted deep throated cheer as it marched past with nearly half a mile of people closely packed on both sides of the road. In most cases the women folk marched ahead, carrying with the upmost comprehensible pride the trophies won during the day. Talk about enthusiasm – the whole village was a surging sea of it. Every face was radiant, there was a happy fire in every eye and in the whole length of Cornwall, I suppose, you would have no such jolly, good-humoured jostling; no such magnanimous comment, no such evident joy of a great day's doings, as those that are characterised by the end of the festival." And so, it has continued to this day. The march down to the contest field with expectations high, the thrill of competition, the tension, as the results are announced and the march back up through the village with the trophies held aloft. It has changed little over the years; the crowds still gather to cheer on their favourites and there are few impartial spectators along the route.

June 1997 saw the Tavistock Town Band attend the Bugle contest for the first time. That year the adjudicator was Goff Richards, a very famous Cornish composer and brass band arranger. We had previously played many of his pieces and it was, indeed, a special day to be able to perform for him. The day, however, was plagued by heavy and prolonged showers. The band played well, beating some bands that were seen as 'firm competition'. These included bands such as Royal British Legion Crownhill Plymouth. These bands ranking a league above us are allowed to enter any section below their own, including ours, the fourth section. We played our best and were awarded fourth place.

Chapter 10 - Building a Band of Ability

"Rhythm and harmony find their way into the inward places of our soul." – **Plato**

It is generally agreed that with a competent Musical Director any band is in with a good chance of growing and attracting new members and certainly over the years Tavistock, like many other bands, had a continual turnover in its members, some good, some bad, but in the main, the vast majority of players were keen players with average musical ability. Some only came to one practice and then disappeared, never to return. Then others stayed for tens of years. We, also saw our fair share of Musical Directors come and go. I'm sure most would have happy memories of their time in the Band. For some reason, we seemed to attract trombone players and Tony Evans was another one. Tony was a professional musician and had a previous career playing in the band of the Welsh Guards.

Band of the Welsh Guards.

A Brass Band is, traditionally, made up of about 25 brass players plus the addition of between one and four percussionists. In the past, we had welcomed anyone willing to commit to attending regular rehearsals and who was reliable to turn up at engagements. Some people had been members for a long time, and although they were not the most proficient players, they were always there and tried their best.

However, after a while, under the baton of Tony Evans, a few things began to change. The overall ability did seem to improve as more competent players joined. The Band became more professional in its approach to how it ran and, also, the types of engagements we took on. No more would the Band consider the small fete type engagement as often the organisers did not even want to pay anything, using the "it's for charity" argument. The Band had a good programme of music and could play to a high standard. Tony found that potential booking clients were, in the main, prepared to pay a fair going rate for our services.

The better the band got the more it seemed to attract players of some ability. Tony aimed to build a band of ability, and his plan seemed to be working. The band had always been a happy band, well in the main. This did not always mix with Tony's more professional stance. No more was it to be a 'come as you please' happy band - it seemed to be turning into a more professional business.

As time went on, more and more new music was purchased. The type of music chosen was the sole responsibility of the Musical Director, and this included deciding on the difficulty level of the music. It seemed clear to me that some of the pieces chosen were beyond the ability of a number of the members. Yes, it is true, all the members could have practised a bit more, especially when they were faced with a piece or passage, they could not play. Unfortunately, the gap between some members' ability and that required to play some of the new music was so great, that some people simply gave up, and so some long-serving members said their 'goodbyes' and left.

As far as many Musical Directors were concerned, Tavistock was considered a happy band, and in the main, they only left due to work commitments or pressures due to their other musical commitments. As soon as it becomes known that a band is doing well and has a Musical Director with leadership or is playing more interesting music, more players are usually keen to join, and it was not too long before new people came to replace those who had left.

The main influx of players came following the breakup of a Plymouth band called Plymouth Crownhill Royal British Legion. This was one of the bands we had beaten at the Bugle Contest previously. They were known for being a staunch contesting band and unlike our band, they had struggled due to 'band politics' and had suffered several breakups and fallouts over the previous years. When several of their players came to join we should have looked ahead a little further. Could anyone have foreseen what was to come?

Ernie Willsher, our much-loved Tuba player.

**Tony Evans leads the band on a very sunny afternoon.
Seen here on the steps of Ilfracombe Bandstand, North Devon.**

At last, Tony Evans was well on the way to achieving his goal. The majority of members were of a good standard of ability. Often attendance at band practice was lacking but it was clear that good players could make a great sound. As the band progressed more and more people wanted to join, and it was here that Tony, perhaps, made a vital error of judgement. Rather than have more members than were required, Tony insisted that numbers be restricted to that specified for contesting. Although this did forego the need to ask or tell members that they would not be able to play at a certain contest, it did mean that if a person was sick, away due to work or other reasons, then the position would not be covered as we carried no surplus numbers.

To be a good brass band, you not only need good brass players but also an able team of percussionists. But at this point, it seemed percussionists did not seem to exist, and we really struggled to attract full time drummers. Tony's solution to this was to use the services of professional percussionist friends from his 'little black book'. On the one hand, this was great as they did not struggle to play the parts, but on the other, the rest of the band has to wait to see how their part fitted with the percussion parts. Of course, it would have been better to have been able to rehearse with the drummers, but this meant extra expense and so was usually avoided. Within about two years, Tavistock had attracted a full team of competent players and now Tavistock had a band of real ability. This was the first time that we played at the Tavistock Carnival without the need to use the services of 'helpers' from other bands. We had our own band, and yes, it felt great marching down the road in a full band, and yes, it sounded good too. But how long would it last and what was all this talk of contesting?

South West Brass Band Association

Chapter 11 - The Glory of Contesting

"Hell is full of musical amateurs." – **George Bernard Shaw** – Irish Playwright

There are many arguments for and against bands taking part in competitions. It is generally considered that taking part will improve the overall standard of your band and encourage better players to join. Yes, the bands in the higher sections can play more difficult pieces of music. They have had to win many contests and competitions to get where they were. Those bands attracted the keen and competent brass band players who were often the real enthusiasts; you know the type that even practiced at home.

But the road to the higher sections is arduous and very long. Brass bands are set out a little like a football league and split into five different sections. At the top is the Championship section, followed by the first, second and third and at the bottom is the entry-level known as the fourth section. Each player can only be registered to play with one band. Unlike concerts, you cannot borrow helpers to fill a gap or boost your team. Players have little card passports with their pictures and signatures on and these are administered strictly by the competition organisers. There would be no way for a band to play on stage with an imposter. All the bands are kept apart in holding rooms or locations within the building and then ushered to the stage when it's their turn to perform. Competitions are staged at large arenas or theatres to enable a large number of players and bands to be kept apart and chaperoned to and from the stage. The adjudicator will have already been ushered under the watchful eye of an administrator to his chair and table which resides, usually in a sort of fabric tent in the middle of the hall. The idea being that they must make their decisions based purely on the sound of the band on stage. They have no idea who is playing, they just have to listen, and try to scribble notes on good and not so good sections within the piece the band on stage is playing. These notes will then be given back to the individual bands, to try to decipher – and you thought Doctor's handwriting was bad?

Each playing band is announced after it has been seated on the stage. The announcer informs the audience what order the band is playing and if it's an own-choice competition, what piece they are to play. At the front of the stage is a large board which shows the order the band is playing and a number which corresponds to the printed programme. Each band is given a number and at no time is it referred to by its name. This way, there is no way for the person in the tent to know which band is playing, he just has to listen. On top of the tent is a system of lights, red and green to show when the adjudicator is ready for the band on stage to start playing, he might also blow a whistle. It's always a little disconcerting to hear silence descend within the hall as everyone waits for the whistle to be blown. Your eyes are firmly on your conductor as you lift your instrument to your mouth and prepare to play. Although you might have been rehearsing the piece for some weeks it's only this one performance that counts. There might be up to twenty bands in your section, and there is a long way between 20th and 1st place.

Since I joined the band, Tavistock had always been in the fourth section, the bottom section. To enable a band to progress to a higher section, it would have to win more than one competition and achieve success time after time. Each band gains points for getting on the prize board, and each year bands can either be relegated, if they are in a section above the fourth, or promoted upwards should they do well. These promotions and relegations are calculated according to the individual bands aggregate placing over the previous three years, so the less a band takes part in competitions, the more difficult it is to gain promotion.

Each part of the United Kingdom has its administrative area and the SWBBA 'The South West Brass Band Association' is in charge of the whole of the South West. This is a massive geographical area which includes Cornwall, Devon, Somerset and Dorset. As well as administering competitions it also collates the points earned by each competing band. The SWBBA also hold their own local Annual Regional Championships and since 1947, these have been held in Torquay & Paignton in Devon. However, in 2022, the competition was held at Cheltenham Race Course as the Riviera Centre Torquay was still being used as a Covid 19 vaccination centre. This competition is open to both members and non-members of the Association.

However, this competition should not be confused with the West of England Regional Championships (also normally held in Torquay) run by WEBBA, the West of England Brass Band Associations. This competition is the qualifying round for bands to go forward to the finals of the National Brass Bands Championships of Great Britain. This is the main competition which culminates with the final at the Royal Albert

Hall, as seen and made so popular in the film 'Brassed Off'. WEBBA is a Council comprised of representatives from the Cornwall, Gloucester, South West [SWBBA] and Wessex Brass Band Associations. Basically, they oversee the whole of the West of England area [which includes the area administered by the South West Brass Band Association [SWBBA]. To add even further confusion, there are various local contests where your band do not earn any points towards the national league tables, but instead has the chance to win trophies and prizes. Playing just for fun, these include contests such as the West of England Bandsmen's Festival also known as Bugle, Exmouth Entertainments Competition [run by SWBBA] and numerous other locally organised competitions such as the 'own choice' Competition held in Weston-Super-Mare. So you can see why contesting can become a little confusing, to say the least.

Below is a table of Fourth Section winners of their local competition. For further information I encourage you to check out their considerable website at; www.southwestbrassbandassociation.co.uk

2022 Bideford Town, Music for a Festival [Mark Durham]
2021 -, - [-]
2020 -, - [-]
2019 Bideford Town Malvern Suite- [Mark Durham]
2018 Redruth Silver Lydian Pictures-[Keith Anderson]
2017 Hatherleigh Silver The Journals of Philias Fogg-[M Green]
2016 Bideford Saddleworth Festival Overture[Mark Durham]
2015 Pendeen Silver English Folk Song Suite -[Daren Jenkin]
2014 Weymouth Concert- Little Suite for Brass No 1-[K Goodwin]
2013 Porthleven Town Partita (Gregson)-[Tom Bassett]
2012 Launceston Town Voices of Youth-[David Dobson]
2011 Launceston Town First Suite in Eb-[David Dobson]

2010 Tiverton Silver Four Cities Symphony [Gilbert Taylor]

2009 Hatherleigh Silver Four Little Maids [David Hayward]

2008 Weymouth Concert Anglian Dances [Adam Glynn]

2007 Sidmouth Town Lydian Pictures [Adrian Harvey]

2006 Pendennis Brass St Michaels Leyline [Steve Thomas]

2005 St Breward Mexican Fiesta [Darren Hawken]

2004 Verwood Concert A Malvern Suite [Paul Norley]

2003 Heyl Town Devon Fantasy [Derek Johnston]

2002 Constantine Silver Little Suite for Brass No1 [Ian Edwards]

2001 Heyl Town Episodes for Brass (Hamner) [Derek Johnston]

2000 St Dennis A Saddleworth Festival Overture [J Berryman]

1999 Lympstone Passing Moods [Charles Fleming]

1998 Lympstone First Suite in Eb [Charles Fleming]

1997 Lympstone Northumbrian Suite [Charles Fleming]

1996 St Breward West Sou'West [WA Hunt]

1995 Pendennis Brass Mexican Fiesta [Glyn Thomas]

1994 St Breward Suite for Brass (Davis) [W Hunt]

1993 Hatherleigh Silver Devon Fantasy [Robin Wonnacott]

1992 Pendennis Brass Swiss Festival Overture [GV Thomas]

1991 Bratton Silver A Malvern Suite [Melvyn Howe]

1990 Porthleven Town Overture to Youth [EF Ralph]

1989 Saltash Town Stantonbury Festival [Roy Jones]

1988 St Gennys Silver Othello [Henry Shipley]

1987 Launceston Town Four Little Maids   [Derek Greenwood]

1986 Bratton Silver West Sou'West [Vic Beer]

1985 Weston-super-Mare Metropolis [Dave Fisher]

1984 Okehampton Excelsior Northumbrian Suite [Reg Beardon]

1983 St Austell B The Seasons [Rodney Richards]

1982 Copperfield Brass A Cotswold Suite [David Tilling]

1981 Torbay Brass English Folk Song Suite [Peter Aunger]

1980 Teignbridge Brass Galantia [Peter Aunger]

1979 Lostwithiel Youth Rufford Abbey [D Howlett]

1978 St Ives Youth Four Little Maids [Eric Toll]

1977 Hatherleigh Silver Wealdon Rhapsody [JMC Nairn]

1976 Sidmouth Town Episodes for Brass (Hanmer) [R Hibbs]

1975 Launceston Town The Lindum Suite [DB Luxton]

1974 Bideford Town A Shakespearean Rhapsody [MW Sweet]

1973 Stoke-sub Hamdon English Country Scenes [W Aird]

1972 Lostwithiel Youth City by the Sea [MW Sweet]

1971 Chard St Michaels Mount [HW Govier]

1970 Lympstone In Switzerland [LR Jennings]

1969 Northlew & Ashbury Spirit of Youth [B Luxton]

1968 Lanner & District Partia Piccola [T Martin]

1967 Junior Leaders Reg Tyrolean Scenes [FL Wilcock]

1966 -, - [-]

1965 Crewkerne Youth A Rural Suite [Mike Shepherd]

1964 Weston-super-Mare A Souvenir of Shakespeare [TS Shearman]

1963 -, - [-]

1962 Boscastle Silver The Golden Age [LR Prout]

The SWBBA is split into regions and the 2022 membership included;

Devon Region Cornwall Region

Appledore Band Bugle Silver

Bodmin TownCamborne Town

Bay BrassLanner & District Silver

Bideford TownRoche Brass

City of Exeter RailwayMount Charles

CreditonPorthleven Town

Devon County YouthSaltash Town

Hartland TownSt Agnes Town

Hatherleigh SilverSt Austell Town

HonitonSt Dennis

South West CommsSt Keverne

Okehampton ExcelsiorSt Keverne Youth

Sidmouth TownSt Pinnock

Soundhouse Brass

South Molton

Tiverton Town

Torbay Brass

Torrington Silver

Somerset Dorset Region

Chard ConcertWeymouth Concert Brass

Glastonbury Brass

Pheonix Brass (Crewkerne)

West Somerset Brass

Weston Brass

Wincaton Silver Brass

Bugle – a pilgrimage for bands

A VIEW from the outside of Bugle Contest would lend weight to the perspective that it is definitely a Cornish event and, although it is open to any band, all the classes are dominated by well established bands bearing old Cornish names.

So, though myself a Welshman, I viewed the contest as a great day out for Cornishmen!

Although it was celebrating its 75th birthday, it was actually the 88th contest as the Festival was first held in 1912 but suspended for the two World Wars, plus there was a one-year break during the recession of the 1930's.

Set on a football field in a small Cornish town with an ideal name for a brass band contest, Bugle has become a pilgrimage for many bands who display a healthy disregard for the end results table or problems caused by player shortages and loyally turn out.

The covered bandstand set in the middle of the Mollinis Park football field is only erected for the day, together with a refreshments tent, under canvas changing facilities, an adjudicator's tent, a portaloo and a gent's loo which was built by the invading Danes in the 8th Century!

Four trade stands, bravely combating the weather, covered their wares with tents hastily constructed from old bits of iron and plastic sheeting which promised very little cover in the event of a heavy downpour and which probably hadn't been called into use since last year's contest.

Chairs for spectators are arranged in a semi circle (15 rows, five deep) around the bandstand and those seasoned Bugle attendees arrived early to overturn their chairs in case it rained; according to most folk it usually does – and it did! Dark clouds hung ominously over the china clay tips, which of course was the main industry of the area alongside the copper and tin mines which survived in Cornwall until the slump in ore prices following the Wall Street Crash in 1929.

Bugle is probably one of the few remaining contests which sees bands march to the field where a prize for best deportment is awarded. From 10am the streets are closed to allow the bands to troop down the hill to the contest field, watched by the hundreds of spectators lining the streets. It is reminiscent of a state visit in London with people calling to their friends, some marching alongside the bands and clapping in time to the music, dogs barking and children simply ecstatic. This then is Bugle, the family day out which spectators and bands enjoy rain or shine, win or lose.

The refreshment tent is a wonder to behold; all the food is home cooked – pastries, sandwiches, Cornish cream teas, cakes and goodies. Add to this wonderful array the helpful, smiling ladies serving who try to tempt you to double your calorie intake 'just for the day' and Bugle is not the place to be!

Tony Evans with the George Collins Trophy

TONY Evans, of Tavistock Band and Maestros Music fame, joined the pilgrimage of bands and enthusiasts who make Bugle Contest their Mecca every year. There are no double figures on offer for competing bands here, just honest to goodness fun for all the family. Here Tony shares his perspective of this old fashioned, unique and beloved band contest which celebrated its 75th birthday two weekends ago.

Some 34 trophies are awarded at Bugle, all displayed throughout the day at the front of the bandstand. The most coveted of these is the Royal Trophy, presented by the then Duke of Windsor and Prince of Wales, and for many years this trophy could only be won by a Cornish band.

I was one of the feisty traders at Bugle, who started the day early with a 30-mile jaunt to set up my trade stand (and tent), not an easy task in the pouring rain. However, I was soon cheered to meet old friends, not least Micky Hunt, the conductor of St Breward Band and Derek Greenwood, with whom I ruminated how well St Keverne were doing; they won the B Class with a band of predominantly young players. Derek and I go back a long way having both served in the Guards and been musical directors of the same band – Crystal Palace.

Many have been returning to Bugle for years; Keith Hammond, my own band's (Tavistock) soprano cornet, is one such Bugle veteran. "It's a great day out and a tradition," he mused. Reward for his staunch support came this year in the form of Best Players Award in the 4th Section.

Another such duo of devotees are Ian and Emma Heard, who met through the Crystal Palace Band, moved into the area and have been supporting Bugle for years. Both feel that it is unique.

Perhaps that is because Bugle is run in an old fashioned way with classes A,B,C and D. There is no big money to be made (or small come to think of it) and the weather can be inclement, even downright inhospitable. But it has a great atmosphere and as I drove away to the strains of the winning top section band playing in the square, taking out of the county the George Collins trophy, lifted by my own band, I agreed silently with my colleagues that there is something special about Bugle. Roll on next year!

At the end of the day, it is the decision of one person, the man in the box, and he might have to listen to up to twenty or even more, with bands often having to play the same piece of music. Yes, some performances will stand out as being particularly good or bad, but having to place in the top three or four is extremely difficult or maybe even just plain 'potluck'. Tavistock played at more and more contests during the next two years, and yes, on the whole, we did very well. It was great to be able to put our trophies on show at our annual 'Last Night of the Proms Concert' (a concert format that perhaps, we started and that is now much copied by many brass bands throughout the country). However, the contests where we did not win a prize or come in the top three bands were quickly hushed up and not discussed. It was not clear if contesting was doing the band any good or not.

Our membership had been stable for some time, but it was clear members from the Plymouth band seemed to be at the fore in pressing for the band to take part in more and more competitions. This had been the main agenda whilst being in the Plymouth band, and they now wanted to continue their obsession using Tavistock. The previous light programme of music seemed to disappear. Tony was not only a lovely person but a very competent musician; however, he was not overly keen to play music that he was not familiar with. Looking to improve himself Tony had recently graduated as Dr Evans from a new University Degree course in 'Brass Band Studies' and he was keen to encourage others in the band to enrol also. However, this seemed to create more and more so-called experts who often at a rehearsal would voice their opinion and even, at times, argue with the Musical Director - had Dr Evans become Dr Frankenstein and had he created a monster of his own?

L – R Chris Northey-Youngs, Peter Hurdwell, Tony Evans,
Adrian Banbury & Ernie Willsher – 'Maestro's Brass Ensemble'

It was around this time that five of us decided to form a Brass Quintet. As Tony was the person who, at that time, provided the music and arrangements. We called ourselves "Maestro's Brass Ensemble" after the name of Tony's music shops. We would meet regularly to play in a smaller group away from the pressures of a large brass band. We soon realised that just as much fun could be had with a smaller group of musicians and this was something that we were to return to in years to come.

The Brass Group had made several commercial recordings, the first of which was on cassette tape at that time. The second recording was a Christmas Album with the Callington Singers. The Brass group also played some pieces without the choir. The CD was recorded in July and a few takes had to be ditched due to an ice cream van going by with its jingle playing at full volume. This was something that we laughed about for many years to come.

I now play with Bideford Town Band, in North Devon and here is their collection of contesting Trophies won in 2022. You see with correct direction, individual practice, along with section rehearsals galore, it is possible to do well in the contesting field, well certainly in the 4th section. Following our success, we were promoted to the 3rd Section. Were we able to play more difficult music arrangements? No. Did we attract more players of a higher standard? No. Did we have a regular team of percussionists who came to more than the odd rehearsal? No. Has much changed in Brass Banding? I would most probably say, not. You see, as a whole 'brass bandies', as players and supporters are affectionately called, are not the sort for any type of speedy change. Some bands even still play the same music we used to play in the seventies. I know we all love a 'good tune', but so much new music is being produced especially for brass bands – come on – get with the 'programme' you 'bandies'!

Bugle West of England Contest 21st June 1997 - Test Piece: A Celtic Suite, Philip Spark

Band Conductor Place Marks

Hatherleigh Silver R. A. Wonnacott 1st 84pts
Indian Queens A. W. McCarthy 2nd 83pts
Penzance E. F. Ralph 3rd 82pts
Tavistock T. Evans 4th 81pts
St. Breward A. Hunt 5th 80pts
RBL Crownhill V. Willcock 6th 79pts

Bugle West of England Contest 19th June 1999 - Test Piece: 1st Suite in E Flat, Gustav Holst

Band Conductor Place Marks

Lympstone C. Fleming 1st 177pts
Tavistock A. D. Evans 2nd 176pts
Penzance Silver F. Ralph 3rd 175pts
Newquay Town V. Roach 4th 173pts
St. Columb Town C. Toghil 5th 172pts
St. Breward Silver W. A. Hunt 6th 171pts
Hatherleigh Silver R. A. Wonnacott 7th 170pts
Torrington Silver M. Reed 8th 169pts
RBL Crownhill V. Willcock 9th 168pts
Pendennis Brass S. Thomas 10th 166pts
Lostwithiel Town G. Swann 11th 164pts

Special Awards

Award Name Band

Best Player K. Hammond (Soprano) **Tavistock Town (Maestro's Music)**

PROGRAMME OF THE
30th WEST OF ENGLAND
BANDSMEN'S FESTIVAL
TO BE HELD AT
BUGLE, CORNWALL
ON SATURDAY, JUNE 19th 1954

Patron: LORD ABERCONWAY
President: SIR JOHN KEAY

VICE-PRESIDENTS—

Rear-Admiral SIR CHARLES E. LAMBE, R.N., C.V.O. (President 1955)
A. BROWNING LYNE, ESQ., J.P., C.A. (President 1932)
A. E. OLD, ESQ. C.A. (President 1947-8-9, 1950-51)

Lady Browning; Hon. Everilda Agar-Robartes; Hon. Violet Agar-Robartes; Mrs. J. R. Cobbold-Sawle; Mrs. M. B. Howell; Mrs A. Michell; Mrs. M. A. L. Jane; Mrs. C. J. Routly; Mrs. H. M. Rowse; Mrs. L. Brenton; Mrs. T. Donovan; Mrs. B. M. Sturtridge; Mrs. W. Tregellas; Mrs. H. Tiddy; Mrs. E. S. Thomas; Miss M. Hawke; Miss K. M. Gilbert; Miss L. Nicholls; Rt Hon. Viscount Clifden, M.V.O.; A. P. Marshall, Esq., Q.C.; W. G. Jerwood, Esq., M.B.E.; Capt. E. Vercoe, O.B.E.; English China Clays, Lovering, Pochin & Co., Ltd.; Bowaters China Clays Ltd.; London Cornish Association; St. Austell Brewery Co., Ltd.; South-West B.B.A.; Holman Bros. Ltd.; N. S. Lyne, Esq., J.P. C.C. Hart Nicholls, Esq; W. T. Nicholls. Esq.; F. Ede, Esq.; J. Y. Hooper, Esq.; F. S. Liddicoat, Esq.; C. Selleck, Esq.; W. R. G Hawke, Esq.; L. P. Mendels, Esq ; C. E. Welsh, Esq.; I. Napier, Esq.; G. Hawke Thomas, Esq.; J. A Atkinson, Esq.; W. J. Batten, Esq ; H. M. Rowse, Esq.; J. H. Trevail, Esq.; J. Tregellas, Esq.; F. Gilbert, Esq.; C. E. Nicholls, Esq.; J. F. Willis, Esq ; G. T. Jane, Esq. M. V. James, Esq ; L. V. Warne, Esq.; R. H. Gould, Esq.; J. Webber, Esq.; E. Crowle, Esq.; W. Coad, Esq.; C. H. Nott, Esq.; H. Jolly, Esq.; T. J. Mewton, Esq.; W. J. Hawken, Esq.; F. G. Blake, Esq.; E. S. Thomas, Esq.; H. Crossman, Esq.; P. C. Tonkin, Esq ; F. Pinch, Esq.; S. Sincock, Esq.; L. Rundle, Esq.; W. J. Wright, Esq.; Capt. F. Dyer; Messrs. Marshalls ; Messrs. Kelly Bros.

HARRY MORTIMER, O.B.E.

Brass and Military Supervisor to the B.B.C. Mr. Mortimer has also had the highest success as Conductor of Contesting Bands. He has adjudicated at the main contests in Great Britain, and the Colonies. Today he Judges this Festival and gives an oral decision on each class.

Festival commences with the National Anthem,

W. & T. Sanders, Printers,

74th Annual Contest
at
MOLINNIS PARK, BUGLE
on
SATURDAY, 20th JUNE, 1998

Adjudicator - James Scott
Deportment Judge - Gareth Roberts MBE

Main Sponsors

Cornwall Snooker Services
ECC International
Rosevears of Bugle
Stephens & Scown, Solicitors
P.C. Tonkin & Son
Whitbread Beer Company

Programme - £1.00

Tavistock Town Band – Contesting Results

Date	Contest	Position	Test Piece	Conductor
25-03-2000	West of England 4th Section	8	The Haslemere Suite	Denzil Stephens
28-11-2000	GBBA March 4th Section	2		A.D. Evans
19-06-1999	West of England 4th Section	2	First Suite in Eb	A.D. Evans
27-03-1999	West of England 4th Section	2	Indian Summer	A.D. Evans
14-11-1998	SWBBA Contest 4th Section	2	Fist Suite in Eb	A.D. Evans
20-06-1998	West of England Class D	6	Overture to Youth	A.D. Evans
04-04-1998	West of England Area Class D	1	Solemn Melody	A.D. Evans
21-06-1997	West of England Class D	4	A Celtic Suite	A.D. Evans
31-03-1990	West of England 4th Section		Summer Fantasy	Ian Whitburn
22-04-1989	West of England 4th Section	12	Suite for Brass (Davis)	Ian Whitburn
05-11-1988	SWBBA Contest 4th Section		Othello	Ian Whitburn
21-03-1987	West of England 4th Section		Overture to Youth	M Kempster
08-11-1986	SWBBA Contest 4th Section		West Sou' West	M Kempster
12-04-1986	West of England 4th Section		Four Impressions for Brass	M Kempster
27-04-1985	West of England 4th Section	27	A Malvern Suite	M Kempster
07-04-1984	West of England 4th Section		Divertimento	L.G. Davis
29-11-1958	SWBBA Contest 3rd Section	1	Melodies for Long Ago	D.J. Carthew
21-06-1958	West of England Class D	4		D.J. Carthew
21-06-1958	West of England Class B	8	Indian Summer	D.J. Carthew
17-11-1951	SWBBA Contest 3rd Section	2	Harmonious Blacksmith	D.J. Carthew
18-11-1950	SWBBA Contest 3rd Section	2	Kenilworth	D.J. Carthew
03-12-1949	SWBBA Contest 3rd Section	2		D.J. Carthew

Home rule for Bugle

This was the scene, late afternoon, at the Bugle contest, when gallons of ice-cream, in addition to a thousand or two Cornish pasties, had been consumed by the large gathering. On the left, MD Howard Taylor leads Bodmin Town (the winners) to the contest field. Below: Derek Greenwood (centre) leads Camborne Town as they march through the village.

AN AWFUL lot of words are being generated in Cornwall on the subject of home rule. It's said that many people are in favour of some form of regional self-government.

There's talk about an assembly along the lines of those being envisaged for both Scotland and Wales.

There are also those who question the sense of such a campaign.

One thing is certain: there was no talk at the West of England Bandsmen's Festival about what home rule would or would not achieve.

Not much changes at Bugle, be it the style of presentation or the people one meets year after year, old bandsmen such as Jim Pinch, Jack Yelland, both of Indian Queens, who were not competing this year, and octogenarian Frank Arthur, still blowing a bass.

Vivian Willcocks, MD of Royal British Legion (Crownhill) Plymouth, couldn't field a full band and went on stage with 19 players. As Mickey Hunt, MD of St Breward, said: "first or last, we're here, and that's what matters."

There was excellent reward for officials and committee who put this splendid contest together, with an entry of six bands in the youth class. A new rule this year allowed a band to play two adult bass players from their senior band, and the change worked wonders.

After a year or two in the doldrums, St Austell appear to be climbing back up the ladder under Len Adams. Working with their youth band is horn player Jane Morford (neé Whitehead), formerly of Sellers, while David Pope has joined the organisation, moving from Mount Charles to assist with

Drum major Jonathon Camps heads deportment winners Bugle as they march in the morning sunshine.

the extra work resulting from the joining forces of the Kernow Band and St Austell.

News of this came not many hours before the contest, which resulted in Graham O'Connor conducting both the senior and junior bands of Mount Charles.

One can stroll around the football field at Bugle and meet people several times during the day, while never catching a glimpse of others. Such as Wesley Wilton. As the bands were marching to the contest field, the news was spreading like wildfire that Wesley, a tireless worker down in the South-West, had been awarded the MBE in the

Birthday Honours. This is for his years of work and effort within the community.

I also met again Douglas Hodge, formerly of Huddersfield and the man who formed and built up Paddock Youth Band, only to see it bite the dust after he moved to St Minver. He's now fully occupied working with the young Camelford Town Band, now 27 strong.

"Some of the youngsters – they were raw beginners about a year ago – have already won prizes at a music festival," he told me, "and I've also started the tradition of church Processions of Witness at Whitsuntide.

"After this year's success it's looking good for next year," he added.

Mentioning Whitsuntide, and John Sharman, a Yorkshireman, now MD of Bugle Band, confessed that this year was the first time he had attended the Whit Friday march contests! "But next year we're looking to take Bugle up there. We're determined not to let Bodmin (regular attenders) have it all their own way."

But what about the matter of home rule for Cornwall?

I bet that if it ever becomes law they'll charge everyone for entering and leaving the county, and not just when you cross the Tamar bridge when heading home.

Chapter 12 - Troubled Times

"Hard times are sometimes blessings in disguise. We do have to suffer, but in the end it makes us stronger, better and wise." – **Anurag Prakash Ray** – *Indian Philosopher*

More and more at rehearsals and even when it came to decision-making, people other than those on the Committee seemed to have a big say about what was decided. I recall the accusations of 'tail wagging the dog', from Chapter 2. The members from the previous Plymouth band seemed to rule the contesting subject because they said they had more experience than everyone else. They had forgotten that at the Bugle contest in 1997 they had come last, and we had come fourth. Also, the people undertaking the Degree course wanted to use the band to practice their conducting skills and to play their new pieces and arrangements. The members who had joined because they wanted to play in a 'good band' pressed for music that they wanted to be played. The remaining members who had been the long-serving people just wanted a happy band that would play good concerts and represent the town. These people, it seemed, now merely got carried along with the flow.

Some of the newer members started to notice that the music programme for our major concerts would change very little from one year to the next. Tony also insisted that at the 'Proms Concert' the choir that should be used must be the Callington Singers. Indeed, the Callington Singers were a very good local choir, but it seemed to many members that our concerts were becoming the 'Tavistock Town Band and Callington Singers show'. The band seemed to be starting to split into distinct factions, and each of these thought their opinion was best. The bane of many a Brass Band, Politics, had now firmly arrived in Tavistock.

Some members began to criticise Tony for not being able to take the band to the next level. The band had gained some success at contesting, but the 'potluck' issue raised its head on many occasions. It seemed that Tony would only choose music that he had played before, and his choice of music for contests was often criticised. More and more people spoke out against him and the way the band appeared to be not progressing. The Band had entered the area championships at the Colston Hall in Bristol, and this was seen as a great opportunity to show people what we could do. Tony was carried along by the people with the loudest voices, and reluctantly agreed that the band should get in a professional conductor to take the band. Tony suggested that his old friend, Derek Greenwood, be asked, but others in the band thought otherwise. The pro-contesting faction preferred professional musician and conductor, Denzil Stephens, and so that was who was commissioned to take the band.

It was around this time that the pro-contest faction seemed to come into its own. They called a meeting at which Tony Evans was asked not to attend. This was unheard of in the whole history of the band – but nonetheless the meeting went ahead. Several people, who were relatively new to the band voiced opinions that were not favourable towards Tony Evans and his ability as a conductor. They felt, perhaps now, he was not the right person to take the band to the next level. Like everyone, Tony did have his limitations - nonetheless such talk was distressing. The pro-contest faction seemed to be taking over. It was decided that Tony be given a period of three months to prove himself. The fact that they had no one to replace him was not really considered. However, a few of the competent players did say they would consider taking on the role of Musical Director. However, these comments were later withdrawn. Obviously, this was not a situation that Tony Evans was to put up with, and he immediately tendered his resignation. This was a sad day for the Band indeed. It was clear that he had created a monster that now turned on him. The band was left with no conductor and a pending important contest. The dark storm clouds were moving in fast.

Cover artwork by Christopher H Northey-Youngs.

Chapter 13 – Denzil Stephens

"Never look at the Trombones, it only encourages them." – **Richard Strauss** *- Composer*

Denzil Stephens was appointed as our contesting Musical Director. Here is an extract from his online obituary following his death in March 2022.

Born in Guernsey in the Channel Isles in 1929, his Salvationist family was evacuated to Yorkshire in 1940, where his musical talent was nurtured. He was soon making a name for himself on the local solo contest circuit, and he was asked to join the Queensbury band at the age of just 15. He was a member of the then Black Dyke Mills bands that secured its first post-second World War 'Area' victory in 1945. He also helped the band win a further 'Yorkshire' title in 1947 as well as a hat-trick of National Championship victories at the Royal Albert Hall between 1947 and 1949. He was, also, a part of the Black Dyke Quartet that won the prestigious British Open Quartet Championship three years in a row.

He stayed with the band until he undertook his National Service in the RAF in 1950, his position as solo euphonium taken by his great friend Geoffrey Whitham, whose family he lodged with. Denzil married his wife, Glenys, in 1950 – a partnership that spanned 52 years. He soon embarked on a successful musical career, able to transfer to the Central Band of the RAF as a euphonium player. His professional skills were enhanced further by lessons with Dr Dennis Wright whilst he undertook the Band Sergeants' Course and Bandmasters' Course winning the Silver Medal for the most outstanding student in 1956.

His first post as a Musical Director was at RAF Bridgnorth, which was followed by becoming a Commissioned Officer in 1959. A peripatetic career evolved – with postings both at home and abroad. He left the RAF in 1978, as a Director of Music. Yorkshire beckoned once more, and he first returned to Carlton Main Frickley Colliery – winning the Granada Band of the Year title in 1978, although he had begun conducting 'civilian' bands as far back as 1968 with the likes of City of Oxford, Rushden Temperance and Grimsby. He had also conducted Cory Band at the Granada Band Competition in 1977, and so, when Major Arthur Kenney left, he was invited to take on the role.

Over the next few years, he reinvigorated them – leading to multiple victories at the Yeovil Entertainment, Pontins, Wembley, Lansing Bagnall and Welsh Championship series and Regional Championships. The band was runner up at the National and European Championships in 1977 and became European Champions for the first time the following year.

Much in demand as a freelance conductor, he also led Swanbrook Transport and Point of Ayr to titles, whilst after leaving Cory he continued to enjoy considerable success with the likes of Lewis Merthyr, BTM and Parc & Dare. He later made a welcome return to Cory leading them to further success in the late 1980s and early 1990s.

Here we can see Denzil with Soundhouse Brass Plymouth on the steps of the Riviera Centre in Torquay at a South West Brass Band Contest in 2005. The band played Philip Wilby's 'Partita for Band – Postcards from Home' and gained 2nd place. I played tenor horn and can be seen above the white arrow.

Returning to live in Cornwall, and having spent some years as Music Editor at Wright & Round, he set up his own publishing company, Sarnia Music, to specialise in his own extensive list of arrangements and compositions, and later a garden supply business in Newquay.

Widowed in 2002, he returned to playing as a member of the South West Tuba Quartet and Bodmin Band as well as taking the baton with local bands such as St Stythians, Mount Charles, Redruth, Soundhouse Brass, Lostwithiel and Tavistock Town Band.

My time spent playing under the direction of Denzil Stephens was indeed, an eye opener, and each rehearsal was nothing less than a master class in how to get the best out of a band of varying abilities. He always made it interesting for those with a greater grasp of their instrument, but those who sometimes struggled were made to feel that their input was just as important. Remember the phrase "there is no 'I' in team", with Denzil it was always about the sound as a collective. "Breath together, sound together, be together". Denzil was indeed a brilliant conductor and always worked hard to get the best performance he could with the resources available.

Denzil Stephens 1929 – 2022 Composer, arranger and life time brass band enthusiast.

Chapter 14 - The Bristol Contest

"I had to leave school at 14 because my father got injured in the mines and I had to support my family. I was an undertaker's assistant, then a plasterer, before doing my military service in the RAF. All the while, I was doing amateur dramatics and dreaming of getting a scholarship to the Bristol Old Vic Theatre School." - **Brian Blessed** - Actor

It was clear at the very first rehearsal that Denzil Stephens was a man of great knowledge and experience. It was made clear by him that the band did contain some good players but the one thing the band could not do was play together as a band. The growing divisions within the band were soon to be highlighted even further. The main part of the new rehearsals was spent playing hymns and slow pieces of music to bring the band together. "No no no....!" Denzil would cry, "listen, listen!" The players who thought they 'knew it all' were soon put in their place. This brought a hidden smile to my face. Perhaps this was something that Tony Evans should have done more forcefully before. After playing through a hymn, he would say "OK, let's do it again, only this time up a tone". Having played piano since an early age, and passed my RSM Grade 8 exam in my early teens, this was not a problem for me. But, a number of players were at a total loss, and again, I laughed to myself. It appeared that these so called 'expert experienced' players did not know as much as they thought they did.

Playing in a brass band will only be effective if everyone has respect for the person out front, the conductor. The whole point is for everyone to play together, as one, often referred to as just one big organ sound.

Everyone is equally important, and it doesn't matter if you are a featured soloist or a tenor horn with the traditional 'oomphs' and middle harmonies, or just a plodding bass line - every part is important. Each player needs to closely observe the conductor and the instructions given both verbally and via his baton, to ensure that everyone is playing at the same tempo. The conductor should not merely be seen as a metronome or someone there just to count the beats and set the tempo. They should have the power through only their hands to shape the music by varying the volume and style within the performance. Normally, small hand movements mean quiet or quieter, and large hand movements mean get louder or loud. A good conductor has to say very little verbally. However, this only works if the players observe the directions given by the conductor. It is a very common practice, in some bands, for players to 'bury their heads in the music' with little attention to the conductor. This is certainly a recipe for total disaster. If you ever get to listen to a Championship section band, then you will notice a crispness and sharp precision in their playing and the conductor will merely shape the performance rather than just beat time.

Denzil Stephens was only able to attend a limited number of rehearsals. Luckily Viv Willcocks, who had previously conducted the Royal British Legion Band Crownhill, Plymouth, offered to take the other rehearsals. Viv was a very able musician who knew what he wanted and worked hard to be able to bring the band together. He was forceful but fair. However, he had stated from the outset that he would not look to take on the role full-time. So, adverts were placed for a new Musical Director who could take the band on a permanent basis.

Unlike previous times when a plethora of people were keen to take on the role, this time, applicants unfortunately did not come flooding in. It seemed, finally, we had even exhausted that supply of baton weilding trombonists. This was strange, as it had often been argued that a band that did well on the contest front, would be more popular, and attract more able players and musicians. Several of the Degree students took turns to hold the baton, but it was clear that they lacked ability due to their limited experience. Given time, any one of them might have been able to fulfil the role, but not at the present time as their inexperience was clear. Conducting might look easy, but it's certainly not just a case of standing out front and waving a stick.

The inside of the old Colston Hall in Bristol as it was in 2000.

The rehearsals with Denzil Stephens continued to highlight problems, and although these should have been relatively easy to correct, things were not that quick to improve. However, by the time the Bristol contest day arrived, the band was able to play the test piece to a high standard. So, on the 25th March 2000, the coach arrived in Tavistock square and the members boarded together with their instruments and a few loyal supporters and family. The thing with contests is that sometimes they never seem terribly well organised. This is, I suppose, mainly because it is uncertain at what time your band will play. There is a draw in the morning to determine the order in which the bands play. Our Chairman, Brian Routledge, drove on ahead to attend the draw.

Brian recalled; "I had previously lived in Bristol for several years and played at the Colston Hall several times and knew the set-up. I arranged a practice hall at Portbury for the morning and then went to the Colston Hall for the draw. I told the band to wait at Portbury for my phone call so they would know when we were playing and also what time we would be allowed to come to the hall because of the limited parking. The next thing I knew was our coach was outside the hall and starting to unload. The organisers ordered us out and I directed the coach to Cannons Marsh car park which I would have done had the band waited for me to return to Portbury. I do not know who decided to alter the arrangements and go direct to Colston Hall."

The entrance to the old Colston Hall Bristol, as it was in 2000.

The Colston Hall in Bristol was built in 1857 as a concert venue and bore the name of prominent local businessman Edward Colston. With its 1950's interior of polished wood and red velvet seats, it was indeed an amazing place to play and ideal for the sounds of Brass Bands. It was one of the Festival of Britain concert halls, along with those on the South Bank, in Coventry and Manchester. It was part of Bristol's contribution to the Festival and, also, of the regeneration of Bristol after the war. The current Colston Hall auditorium is the fourth on the site after fire destroyed previous ones. The most recent fire, started by a cigarette in 1945, gutted the building. So, while the exterior dates from the turn of the century, the interior was entirely rebuilt in Festival style in 1950-1 by Bristol city architect J Nelson Meredith – and very fine it was too. When it opened in 1951, the same year as the Festival Hall, Meredith's interior, devised in partnership with the eminent acoustician Hope Bagenal, was considered one of the best of the Festival of Britain era in both acoustic and design terms. It did sound like you were playing by yourself on that huge stage and you had to listen like mad to ensure you were together with the other players. The very first time playing in there was, to say the least, very disconcerting, if not totally horrifying.

2000 the inside of the old Colston hall – all of this, including the light fittings and ceiling, have now been removed following the refit which concluded in 2020 costing £107m, way in excess of the budgeted £52.2m.

The hall had been built to seat an audience of 2,000 and a choir of 182, within the shell of the Victorian building. Despite those constraints, it was a well-proportioned space and had good acoustic standards. The fittings and furnishings were simple but of fine quality. The side walls were panelled in chestnut veneer detailed with strips of Mansonia (a hardwood from West Africa) and a Mansonia dado. The front of the auditorium had hardwood flooring of Muhuhu (from East Africa), so it could be used for dancing or exhibitions. It is remarkable that such exotic woods, imported from around the British Empire, were used at a time of post-war austerity when materials were scarce and expensive.

The previous 1936 design by C F W Denning included a deep balcony so that the hall could be used as a cinema. This had been reinstated and was decorated with plaster motifs by Ernest Pascoe. The hall still had its original insulated doors, with their distinctive porthole windows, and the stylish original light fittings. It also had a bespoke movable boxing ring, which was designed to fit partly on the platform and partly on the floor of the auditorium, with competitions held in it until the mid-1990s.

A copper-clad foyer building, designed by Levitt Bernstein, was added to the Hall in 2009. The site was given a £107m refurbishment which concluded in 2020 with the hall being renamed the Bristol Beacon following the 'Black Lives Matter' demonstrations which highlighted the fact that its original namesake, Edward Colston, had gained much of his wealth from the slave trade.

After arriving at the venue for our long-awaited Bristol competition it was soon our turn and we all made our way to the stage. We went on and sat down looking around at the huge auditorium and the ceiling that looked as if it was a mile away. Denzil appeared and we waited for the adjudicator to blow his whistle from within his little sealed tent, to indicate that we could commence our performance of Peter Graham's 'Haslemere Suite'. It consisted of four separate movements, Haslemere Town, Beside the Way, Waverley Abbey and Charter Fair. Each movement has a different style and sound and is, therefore, designed to test the entrants; featuring some solos to test the leading instruments of each section. We played our very best for our man in the middle, Denzil. It was a fair performance, but you only get one chance so all we could do now was to wait in anticipation for the results.

Colston Hall Bristol now renamed Bristol Beacon.

Around this time, the fourth section was a popular contesting forum and there were often over twenty bands playing. After securing our instruments, members went into the main auditorium to listen to some of the other bands perform. But even after only listening to a few bands play, most were bored of listening to the same piece over and over again and retired to the bar area. Perhaps, now we could appreciate what the man in the box was going through.

It had, previously, been decided that the coach would leave at a predetermined time. Unfortunately, when this time arrived the results still had not been announced. Some people later said they were not happy that we had to leave before we knew the result. But, unfortunately, they did not voice this opinion until later. Anyway, the coach was ready to leave and so, we returned to Tavistock and awaited a call from a few members who had travelled up in their cars and who stayed for the evening concert and, of course, the results. The call came and announced that we had come 8th out of the 29 bands that had played. Not a bad result, by any means, and the result should have been greeted with celebrations however, this was not the case.

I recall that the next band practice was a little strange, and certain members did not seem happy with the result. They, evidently, thought we should have done better. Furthermore, "why did the coach leave before the results? – they roared!" Again, the chap in the box 'did not have a clue - he was an idiot'. Following the results being announced at a contest, each band is given a written sheet by the adjudicator which details his comments and suggestions concerning our performance. These normally contain a mixture of positive comments and also, observation of bits that, perhaps, could have gone a little better. Ours was examined in great detail by those 'who knew.' Each negative comment was disputed and argued with. Some members tried to remind them of the 'pot-luck' theory and that our result should be celebrated, but these comments did not seem to hold much water. Not having been a person who ever followed football, I could now see why some football supporters, sometimes get very upset. After all, it's supposed to be 'fun' right?

We now found ourselves with an unhappy band with no Musical Director and a full diary of summer bookings and of course, let's not forget the date of our annual 'Proms Concert' in September which was also fast approaching. What was going to happen with Tavistock's fine contesting band of ability now?

The river Tavy runs through the heart of the town of Tavistock, and it's where the town gets its name from. Here we can see the weir just off Bedford Square, in the centre of the town, with the water running away as fast as our band's luck.

Chapter 15 - The Snowball Effect

"The English may not like music, but they absolutely love the noise it makes." – **Thomas Beecham** - *Conductor*

It was clear that we had to get things sorted. The previous conductor of Plymouth Royal British Legion, later to become 'Soundhouse Brass' Viv' Wilcocks had again offered to hold the position of Musical Director but only for a while. He made it very clear that he would not be able to help the band at the weekends. This was obviously a problem, as of course this was when the majority of our bookings were for, so for a few weeks, some of the more knowledgeable and experienced members tried to help select a programme of music and also took some practices.

It was soon time for the band's annual general meeting. It was held as usual on a rehearsal night to maximise attendance. For some reason, all some members wanted to talk about was the Bristol contest. Many people voiced their opinion and said they were very unhappy with the result and that we should have done much better. Tensions were high, and people seemed to dwell unnecessarily on the past rather than looking to the future and getting things sorted. Some members had harsh comments for the group led by our committee Chairman, Brian Routledge, who had organised the coach and the rehearsal premises at Portbury. Again, people continued to talk about the past, and not to mention what they called 'the fiasco about the coach leaving before the result was announced', as if that would have made any difference to the result. At the end of the Chairman's report, Brian Routledge said that he too had been unhappy for some time and tendered his resignation. With that, he got up and left the meeting and has not been seen from that day to this. This was, to say the least a bit of a shock. Things like this did not happen in Tavistock Town Band. When no one stepped forward to assume the role of Chairman the meeting disbanded without a committee being appointed. It was agreed that things would be concluded at the next band practice. People had clearly had enough for one night.

At the next meeting, a rather shaky committee was appointed, and an even shakier practice followed. Things were very unstable, and tensions continued to run high. It seemed to remind me of my first time trying to play while sitting on a child's chair on the cobblestones in the stable of the Market Inn back in the 1970s. Things to say the least were a little 'wobbly'.

During the next few practices more and more people left. The people who had gained their music Degree's studying the brass band course with Tony Evans all left en mass. Some who had allegiance to Brian and Tony also left along with some previously regular 'helpers'. Members said that they did not want to play in a band that did not have a full complement. But as more and more left this situation became more and more evident. Then we found ourselves left with only a few players, maybe only five. We sat around and looked at each other in disbelief. What were we going to do? We had enough members still to be able to keep going according to the band's rules and constitution. We were even able to form a definite committee, with each remaining person holding a position. I remained as Treasurer. It was strange that the people who were left were the original members who had seen the others come and go. We could not help thinking that perhaps we were to blame.

We continued to advertise for a Musical Director, but the replies were few and far between. We rehearsed in a large hall at Mount House School in Tavistock but retained our premises in the basement of the Council chambers in the centre of the town, primarily for storage. As time went on more and more members left and the band got smaller and smaller, and the hall seemed to get bigger and bigger. The clock was ticking as the date of our annual 'Last Night of the Proms' Concert loomed closer and closer. Our audiences would not be that impressed with a Quintet of musicians trying to play the finale pieces which were expected at our concert. What were we going to do?

Chapter 16 - The Proms Project

"Suddenly a mist fell from my eyes and I knew the way I had to take." – **Edvard Grieg** – *Composer*

We were left with a nucleus of about ten players. The South West Brass Band Association encouraged an older gentleman, known as John, to come and take the band. I can't remember his surname, but I can remember his black briefcase that accompanied him at all times. The remaining players had suggested a few pieces that we thought we could perform. John did not agree with the pieces chosen and so decided, as was within his rights as temporary Musical Director, to choose some other pieces - and so rehearsals began. Thinking back, I think he just wanted to assert his position from the outset.

After a few weeks, John said that he sensed that, perhaps, he did not have the total support of the group before him. This was not strictly true as we saw him as our potential saviour and, although not everyone agreed with his choice of the music programme the decision on musical content was his. During rehearsal, we often had a break, primarily a tradition to keep the smokers happy. On one particular occasion, a few members tried out an arrangement by one of the cornet players, Peter Hurdwell. John saw this as a dig and threat against his authority and threw his baton into his black shiny briefcase, turned around and left. You can see how brass bands and politics are often mentioned within the same sentence. Our main annual concert was looming and, again, we were left with no Musical Director. Things seemed to be going from bad to worse.

By now I had been in the Band for some 25 years, and therefore, decided to take personal responsibility, for seeing through a special project to enable the 'Proms Concert' to go ahead. It was also my aim to make this the best 'Proms Concert' yet, and to ensure the survival of the Band into the new millennium. We looked to our fellow local bands for support to help take the project forward, and we gained support from members of Stannary Brass in Tavistock, Callington Town Band and a few from Saltash Town Band. At last we were starting to 'Band together'.

The 'Last Night of the Proms' themed concert had been devised some years previously and it always seemed to be well received. As well as the brass band, we would invite other musicians to take part to ensure the audience had a varied musical programme as well as the opportunity to sing the famous finale pieces of 'Land of Hope & Glory', 'Sea Songs', Jerusalem and 'Rule Britannia'. Rehearsals began in earnest with me holding the baton. The band's programme was finalised having received the members' consent. Light but effective pieces were chosen with the majority of the work being done on the finale pieces. Rehearsals went well and it seemed to remind me of my early days in the band when the music and having fun was the main priority and not what someone else sat in a box thought.

We gained the support of local Soprano Rosemary Turner. Rosemary had been my music teacher at Tavistock Comprehensive School. Also, the Chamber Choir of Tavistock College and a local harpist, Abigail Pine, offered their services, together with a local classical string trio. The chorus for the finale would consist of members from the Tavistock Musical Theatre Group.

Our 'Last Night of the Proms' Concert at Tavistock Town Hall with Simon Badge conducting.

As September approached, a finely tuned advertising campaign was put into operation and tickets sold like hotcakes. Everyone was given a job to do, unlike on previous occasions when it was left to the few. Well to be truthful, the actual remaining members of Tavistock Town Band were the few. There was a lot to coordinate to ensure everyone taking part knew how long they were to play for, as it was important the concert started at 7.30 pm and concluded by, at the latest, 10.00 pm. This was to be our biggest concert, perhaps ever, and we could not turn away supporters who were keen to help us. A large poster for the advertising frame outside the town hall was made, and I must admit it looked impressive.

The night of the Concert arrived. The hall was decked with bunting streamers and flags. The podium was in place and the audience began to arrive. Our friends from the theatre group together with friends and family of band members were recruited to help ensure the raffle and everything ran smoothly. The concert began on time, and everything was fine. The audience was responsive to the patter I had prepared, and we ensured that audience participation would far outrank that of previous years. Our friends and fellow groups and artists performed to an appreciative audience and the final chorus of 'Land of Hope and Glory' and 'Jerusalem' almost lifted the roof of the Town hall.

At the end, everyone helped to dismantle the bits and pieces, the flags, the bunting and we all sat down for a well-earned rest. The question on everyone's lips was - what were we going to do now?

Rosemary Turner sings 'Rule Britannia', and yes, she made her own festooned red, white and blue dress from Union Jack flags.

Chapter 17 - Tavistock Pro Brass

"Works of art make rules; rules do not make works of art." – **Claude Debussey** - *Composer*

The Proms project had worked far better than anyone had ever imagined. But, we still had less than ten members no Musical Director and no clear vision of what to do next. Strangely, our remaining members were all long-term members who had been with the band for some time. These included; Peter Hurdwell, Robin Clowes, Mark North, Darrell Alexander, myself and our long-standing tuba player, Ernie Willsher. With such a small group we could not really spare one of us to be our Conductor. Then we were thrown a potential lifeline, when a shining beam of hope appeared in the form of an idea by our past Musical Director, Dr Tony Evans. Despite, previously, being forced to resign from the band, Tony was a good friend and professional musician, and he was keen to see something he too had loved survive and move forward.

Tony's idea was to have a meeting of all interested parties to form a large brass ensemble of competent musicians to take forward a condensed band, for the town of Tavistock. The meeting took place at the Royal British Legion Club in Tavistock, and plans were outlined, but these did not include the resurrection of Tavistock Town Band as people insisted that the new group would be different. This was fine with the remaining members, and it was agreed that assets from the band be lent to the new group to plan a Christmas Concert in Tavistock Parish Church. We would also financially assist with any costs involved, and this was seen as being fine to support a venture that could potentially lead to a larger ensemble or even in time the reformation of a full brass band for Tavistock.

His idea was to have a group of no more than ten or so competent musicians who Tony knew, personally from previous times. The group met for its first rehearsal and the grand plan was outlined. We would start with a Christmas Concert, and see how things went from there. His plan of playing without a conductor soon fell by the wayside, as it became clear that even experienced musicians needed some direction from the front. The fact that we only had a few players, meant that should absence raise its head due to work, illness and the usual excuses for not attending rehearsal, we would struggle to have effective meetings, as in a smaller group, taking even one person out was a greater percentage than in a band of thirty. But, as it turned out, attendance was good, on the whole, and rehearsals continued in earnest. Unfortunately, our solo trumpet player, Norman, was I think, a farmer, and he missed more than a few rehearsals over the coming weeks.

An article appeared in the Tavistock Times where Tony was quoted saying – 'We have the services of Norman Pendray, who is one of the finest cornet players in Cornwall, plus other players of a good standard. Our concert will have support from Plymouth's latest jazz duo Colla Voce, ex-Welsh National Opera Soprano, Elaine Rockell and Mary Tavy harpist, Abigail Pine. We can guarantee a concert like nothing heard in Tavistock for some time. But, following the success of our 'Last Night of the Proms' concert only a few months before we knew we had a lot to live up to.

Rehearsals proceeded, but in retrospect, it was clear that things were not progressing as fast as Tony may have liked. The date of the Christmas Concert arrived, and Tavistock Pro Brass was launched to a much smaller, yet appreciative audience than in previous years. The concert went well but it did nothing to come even close to the spectacle of our recent 'Proms Concert'. Our audiences were used to coming to concerts in the Town Hall, and even though the Parish Church was only a matter of yards across the road, numbers were noticeably less than we would have expected. This was a shame as the acoustics of the church is far superior to that of the Victorian Town Hall. The sounds produced were angelic, to say the least, and our limited audience reported that they had enjoyed the music content and that it was, definitely, value for money, it was just such a shame that only a few people turned up.

Afterwards, the group packed up its music stands, banners and equipment, carrying everything across the road to our band room in the basement of the Council Chambers in Drake Road and, unfortunately that was the end of Tavistock Pro Brass. The potential draw of having one of Cornwall's top cornet players had not proved the draw that Tony thought it would. At the time I was a member of a private members' social club in Tavistock called the West Devon Club and the nucleus of players went with me for a well-earned drink, and this was where a new idea was born, a new idea, a brilliant idea, something that, perhaps, we should have thought of a long time ago - it was a real light bulb moment.

The West Devon Club – A Tavistock private members club.

Chapter 18 - Tavistock Versatile Brass Ensemble - T.V.B.E.S.

"You have to trust that the dots will somehow connect in your future... The only way to do great work is to love what you do. If you haven't found it yet, keep looking. Don't settle. As with all matters of the heart, you'll know when you find it... Have the courage to follow your heart and intuition. They somehow already know what you truly want to become. Everything else is secondary." – **Steve Jobs** – *Entrepreneur, business magnate, media proprietor and co-founder of Apple.*

As the remaining members of the town band sat drinking lemonade in the bar of the West Devon Club, we thought about the concert we had just performed and tried to analyse why this venture had not worked. We decided that having professional players was not any better than us if they did not turn up to rehearsals. After all, it was only if we could rehearse as a team that the band would sound together. We had learnt from the 'Last Night of the Proms' concert the previous September that you did not have to play complicated or difficult music if you chose the pieces well. Audiences simply do not appreciate a more difficult piece versus something they can tap their toe along to or a tune they have heard before, perhaps on the TV or in a film. We thought how many players do you need to be able to 'bang out' a good tune? We decided that you could most probably get away with as little as two trumpets [cornet] a horn for the middle part, a tuba for the bass part, a trombone for the tenor line and a euphonium or baritone for the melody or counter melody.

So, the remaining members decided that we would form our own brass ensemble. This would not be a separate venture but a natural evolution of Tavistock Town Band back to its very original roots. At the opening of Tavistock Town Hall, a small brass ensemble had played and now we had gone full circle returning to this original format. We had gone wrong previously because we had tried to keep going with a type of musical group that was not conducive to the times we were living in and the limited resources available to us. We needed something that would work with the talent and ability that was at hand. It was going to be a group for 2001 and beyond. We were so pleased with our decision, that we got another round of drinks in and sat to celebrate our idea, and to discuss how we would move things forward.

The new group met in January 2001 and consisted of two trumpets which included Peter Hurdwell, a horn, myself, Chris Northey, a tuba, Ernie Willsher, a euphonium, Mark North a baritone horn, Robin Clowes and a trombone, Darrell Alexander. We pondered over a name for our group -

but all became clear when we talked about the objectives of the group. We did not want to be the remains of a brass band, we wanted to be our own thing. We decided we would aim to play music that we enjoyed playing and that hopefully, people would enjoy listening to. We would play brass music for the locality and, also, look in time to represent the town of Tavistock further afield. We wanted to illustrate that even a small brass group or ensemble could play a variety of different types of music and be truly versatile. Being a much smaller group, we would look to perform at functions where the numbers of a full brass band would, perhaps, not work, events such as weddings, fetes, bandstands and seafront concerts. After all, Tavistock had one of the best purpose-built band stands in the area, the acoustic was great, and the sound could be heard throughout the river Tavy valley. Tavistock Versatile Brass Ensemble known locally as TVBEs was born.

Luckily, we had retained our practice room in the basement of the Town Council Offices, Drake Road, and rehearsals went well. For the vast majority of rehearsals, we had one hundred per cent attendance. For all of us, this was something new and very exciting. We were lucky to have very talented members who could not only play various instruments but could also arrange music, especially for the group and the particular complement of instruments. For me, the chance to write and arrange music was great. We often had new music to play, and these were pieces and arrangements specifically written not only for the instrumentation we had but also for the ability of each player. Our venture had the blessing of Tony Evans and he even donated arrangements for us to play. We had something that no one else had. We were unique. Summer 2001 saw our first public performances. We were lucky enough to pick up engagements that had previously been done by the brass band and this soon got us noticed and the bookings came flooding in. We played at fetes and private functions such as weddings and even a birthday party. If we felt like it, we would go down to the park and set up at the bandstand and play for the afternoon, this was a Sunday afternoon regular concert. Because we were such a small group we could make snap decisions with ease, and remember this was a time before the social media we have today. We had no 'Facebook Messenger' or 'WhatsApp' we just made and agreed on decisions between us at rehearsals. It was easy and worked well, we were I suppose, our own unofficial committee.

Tavistock Town Council Offices, which for many years housed our rehearsal premises in the basement.

Playing a Christmas Concert at the 'Great Barn' Buckland Abbey.

Playing at Tavistock Vintage Steam Fair.

Summer 2013 – Open Gardens Charity Event Gunnislake.

The bandstand in Tavistock's Park, known as the Meadows, is particularly good for smaller groups as the acoustics are most effective, especially if the people playing can all be as near the centre as possible. It was built by Victorian architect Sir Edwin Lutyens. After beginning his own practice in the late 19th century, Lutyens played a key role in designing and building New Delhi and was responsible for many famous buildings and monuments here in the UK, including the Cenotaph in London's Whitehall, and Devon's Castle Drogo.

The Bandstand, during the s1970's had a secret compartment underneath that housed a supply of folding metal chairs with wooden slatted green seats. Unfortunately, over time these began to deteriorate and at some stage, the hidden door was sealed forever. Perhaps the chairs are still in there? Thanks to a quick trip to Cornwall's famous 'Trago Mills' we purchased about ten wooden folding chairs which were perfect for easy transportation and use at venues such as the bandstand and playing Christmas Carols in the street in December.

Tavistock Lutyens Bandstand in Tavistock Park [the Meadows].

Another particularly good concert was performed at the millennium bandstand in Kingsbridge and also in Ilfracombe on one of the hottest days of 2001. Tavistock's Band was back! And we were having fun. Who needed thirty-five people and a committee?

The Millennium Bandstand in Kingsbridge 2001.
Unfortunately, this was set alight and burnt down by vandals on 23rd January 2023.

The stability of the group was heart-warming indeed, following the past few years of trouble and uncertainty. The 2001 'Last Night of the Proms' concert was organised with ease, having learnt much from the previous year. The main part of the concert was performed with the assistance of Saltash Town Band who was South West champions at the time. Tavistock Versatile Brass Ensemble, TVBEs performed four pieces to illustrate the true versatility of a small brass group. We were warmly received. It was then that we finally knew that the format we had chosen for the group was going to work - and work well. Who needs the expense and hassle of a large brass band, when a small brass group can generate so much more enjoyment, both playing and hopefully listening?

2009 charity presentation £1873

2010 charity presentation £1682

2012 charity presentation £1000

2013 charity presentation £2000

2014 charity presentation £1516.62

December saw a busy carolling programme raising funds for local Cancer charities, something the group continued to do in subsequent years. We have managed to raise thousands of pounds for charity since the group started in 2001. As we made money from performing other concerts throughout the year, every single penny collected during our Saturday morning carolling each December was given to our chosen charity.

Not even snow stopped us from playing Christmas Carols and collecting for our charities. Here we can see band supporter Simon Prout.

Dave Dobson Conducts Tavistock Versatile Brass Ensemble (TVBEs) at a Christmas Craft Fair at the Great Barn, Buckland Abbey, Devon. This smaller group was perfect for playing at such venues. Although I remember it was very cold, even inside. The huge expanse of the barn meant it was impossible to heat, and the fact that the windows and openings had no glass, and the doors, although large did little to keep the icy wind out, it resulted in a chilly afternoon. The complimentary mulled wine and warmed mince pie during a break from the music was most welcome. We had just enough players to be able to play some of my own arrangements of traditional Christmas tunes which were always well received. The mix of instruments was perfect.

Me doing my daily practice on Bideford Quay, North Devon, December 2021.

Chapter 19 – Concentrating on Making Music

"Music is healing. Music holds us together." **Prince** - *Musician*

Between 2001 and 2014, Tavistock Versatile Brass Ensemble (TVBEs) performed at many local events in and around the town of Tavistock. Each December we worked hard and raised funds for local Cancer charities by playing in the main street, come rain, come shine. With the town being on the edge of Dartmoor, some Decembers were even plagued with heavy snow.

We enjoyed performing whenever we wanted to in the bandstand in the park and each September to coincide with the BBC Last Night of the Proms event we continued our annual concert using a tried and tested format. We were a very happy band.

We moved our annual main concert from Tavistock Town Hall to the town's Wharf Theatre, mainly due to the fact the Theatre had a Box Office and offered more advertising (not that we ever had anything less than a full house). We performed together with a Brass Band, using the services of bands such as Saltash Town Band, Soundhouse Brass & Bodmin Town Band. We, also, were very fortunate to have the support of talented local Sopranos Rosemary Turner and Kate Walker to sing the solo role in 'Rule Britannia'.

Tickets always sold out in advance and people came ready with their flags and increasingly elaborate, red white and blue costumes. They were always assured of a great evening of entertainment, music and a very rousing finale to the tune 'Rule Britannia!'

Other vocalists and groups were keen to join in with our concert, not only to be able to play to a large audience but also to enjoy the fantastic atmosphere of the event each year. Our friends included Simon Prout, Tyron Piper, Jane Distin, Julian Bennett and Peter Clement and choirs included 'Tavistock Musical Theatre Company' Chorus, 'Callington & Gunnislake Circuit Methodist Choir', The 'Carmenians Theatre Company' Chorus, 'Devo Cantare', 'Canoryon Lowen', Tavistock's 'Vocal Harem & the Sultans of Sing', The 'Rob Young Singers', 'Young at Heart' and the 'Sterts Singers' - to name but a few.

In 2011 we moved the main concert to Sterts Theatre at Upton Cross near Liskeard, Cornwall. Due to the stage size and the larger arrangements written especially for the group, we would often invite extra players to join us. Due to our increased numbers, we would also invite a conductor to aid our performance. Our first Conductor was Simon Badge, someone who I had played with, previously in the Soundhouse Brass Band when he played tuba. He was a great supporter and always looked very impressive stood out front in his Royal Marine uniform. Another great friend of the group and our next real long-term Conductor was Dave Dobson, a man of great musical experience and someone with a real passion for the music of brass bands. I had first played under his baton as a member of Saltash Town Band many years before and was aware of his musical ability. Dave and his wife Julie were to become long-term friends.

Our Sterts Theatre 'Last Night of the Proms' played every year to packed houses. The larger space enabled us to put on larger scale performances, which often included pyrotechnics, lighting effects and full-scale musical theatre numbers with a cast of up to thirty people or so – quite a spectacle. Sterts was originally an outside amphitheatre before being enclosed with a huge canopy structure, which, at least, provided some shelter from the frequent wet Bodmin Moor weather. It also enabled us to increase our ticket number to over 400 seats which proved worthwhile financially. We were, actually, making money!

Our 'Proms' concerts were always assured of being a 'sell-out'.

Although we had no intention to return to the format or numbers of a brass band, the popularity of our music and our relaxed rehearsal environment and focus on playing new and exciting music, meant that, often, our concert helpers would remain and so our number started to grow from our original quintet to a much larger brass group. We enjoyed playing contemporary music which originated in America. Unlike here in the UK, American schools give every pupil the opportunity to learn a musical instrument, hence the large number of school bands, orchestras, marching bands and other musical groups which drive such a thirst for new and exciting music. Our modern music programme proved ever popular with our members and audiences alike. The stuffy brass band music was long gone.

Our concerts at 'Sterts' allowed us to put on a real show!

I was lucky to have a friend who lived in America and he helped us quickly build a library of completely new music. Due to the internet, it is easy to purchase new music scores and individual parts. This made our group completely original and very different compared to anything else in the locality. A particular feature of our music was the involvement of percussion. We had a team of six regular percussionists who greatly added a further dimension to our music.

**Our initial percussion Team L- R
Richard Barbery
Rachel Hutty
Nick Anderson
Will' Bennett**

I was Master of ceremonies for all our concerts.

May Concert - Tavistock Parish Church 2012. *

2012 saw the passing of our friend and long-standing Tuba player Ernie Willsher. Ernie had been a main-stay of the band for as long as I could remember, also a very efficient Librarian, roadie and good friend to us all.

Annual Charity Christmas Collection December 2009. *

Our concert posters were always colourful and eye catching.

2010 to 2014 saw a considerable investment in expensive percussion equipment including a huge gong, pedal timpani drums, xylophones and orchestral tubular bells to name but a few. It soon became clear as our

numbers expanded that our percussion team was just as important as the brass players. Our very healthy membership included 3 trombones, 3 French horns, 2 euphoniums, a tuba, a healthy number of trumpets and 6 percussionists.

Our Sterts theatre shows often included full theatrical numbers, complete with singing and dancing.

Playing the 'Hoedown' 'Hootenanny' required that we also wore costumes.

It soon became clear, that with our membership numbers increasing beyond the initial Quintet, that it would not be possible for me to play and conduct. So, the group was pleased to be able to invite our friend Dave Dobson to become our next full-time conductor. This was excellent news as it enabled us to play more and more complicated pieces of music. Our music source in America helped us by providing ever increasing complicated music which featured our new percussion equipment. Our sound and make up was again transforming from a few brass band friends to a full orchestral brass ensemble.

Dave Dobson appointed as Associate Conductor.

By 2012 we had grown in numbers considerably. This was mainly due to the fact that more and more people wanted to come and play the type of music they had heard us play in the concerts during the previous few years. This was music and arrangements that simply were not heard anywhere else in the country. Our contacts in the states had really done us proud, introducing us to a wealth of music being written today for school wind bands and marching bands in American schools. Our education system really needs to take a leaf from their book. Only just this week, the band I now play in has brought out a piece to the music folders, which I have been playing since I was in a brass group at school. I'm not saying there is anything wrong with that but, it would be refreshing to look forward rather than back, and that's something we did all the time in our brass group, Tavistock Versatile Brass Ensemble 'TVBEs'.

May Concert - Tavistock Parish Church 2012.

2012 May Concert with the previous cornets now replaced by trumpets to create a brighter more orchestral sound. Tavistock Parish Church has an ideal acoustic for brass.

Last Night of the Proms 2013 [below] Sterts Singers and guest Soprano Soloist Kate Walker.

Our Pirates of the Caribbean selection included our own Jack Sparrow [Richard Barbery].

My good friend, Julie Dobson, with our guest Bodmin Town Band.

Daphne Dunce, the Dowager Duchess of Doublebois & Duke Denzil Dipwitt of Darleyford also graced us with their presence.

Chapter 20 – Tavistock Rhythm & Brass

"The wise musicians are those who play what they can master." - **Duke Ellington** – *American Pianist*

In 2014 we chose to modernise our image and name by illustrating the importance of our percussion members, and changed our name to 'Tavistock Rhythm & Brass'. I designed our new logo to comprise our group initials and the traditional town colours of red and black, this harked back again to the colour of our previous brass band uniform colours. We purchased a set of quality red shirts and arranged for them to be embroidered locally, with the new name and logo. Everyone agreed we all looked very smart. It reminds me of the black and white photos of Brian Routledge and Mike Cole in their new black, red and gold band uniforms from the 1950's [see previous chapters].

By now Tavistock's Town Band had become a stable group of friends

who enjoyed meeting up to play interesting and original music, as well as some of the old favourites. The band met every Friday evening and sometimes an additional Sunday morning in the same band room in the basement of the Town Council Chambers, Drake Road, Tavistock. A great place to rehearse as it gave us a large room to practice in that was effectively below ground [although it did have windows thanks to a small courtyard outside, but with no access from the street level above]. We also had a storeroom which was great to keep unused instruments, uniforms and four filing cabinets which housed a full brass band library as well as our own brass group music. The most important words in this paragraph are that we were all 'friends' and this is an important thing to bear in mind as we approach the end of our story in a few chapters time.

Following the change of the group's name to Tavistock Rhythm & Brass [Tavistock R&B] we found ourselves concentrating much more on music and arrangements which, equally, included percussion. We had managed to sell our old and unused library of brass band music to a newly founded brass band from the Midlands. This generated a welcome pot of cash to augment the items already in our percussion team. We were lucky, not only, to have such kit as expensive tubular bells, tam tams [gong], xylophone, glockenspiel, new pedal timpani and various drums and bits to rattle but also people who could play them, and, more importantly, they regularly attended rehearsals.

There were no other groups in the area that had the task of putting a set of tubular Bells in the boot of your car to trek to Plymouth to play Christmas Carols in the city centre. Everyone enjoyed playing in our group and our future seemed strong and secure – what could possibly go wrong?

Our American contact did well to introduce us to new composers, arrangements and new pieces that made our band unique. Our concerts now included film music and atmospheric pieces that included choirs and pianos & keyboards. We ensured we always had a balanced programme of music which our audiences gave us great feedback on. Our membership had grown and even included a full set of French horns. I played in Plymouth University Orchestra and players from there were keen to come and be included in some of our concerts, and we were very pleased to have them.

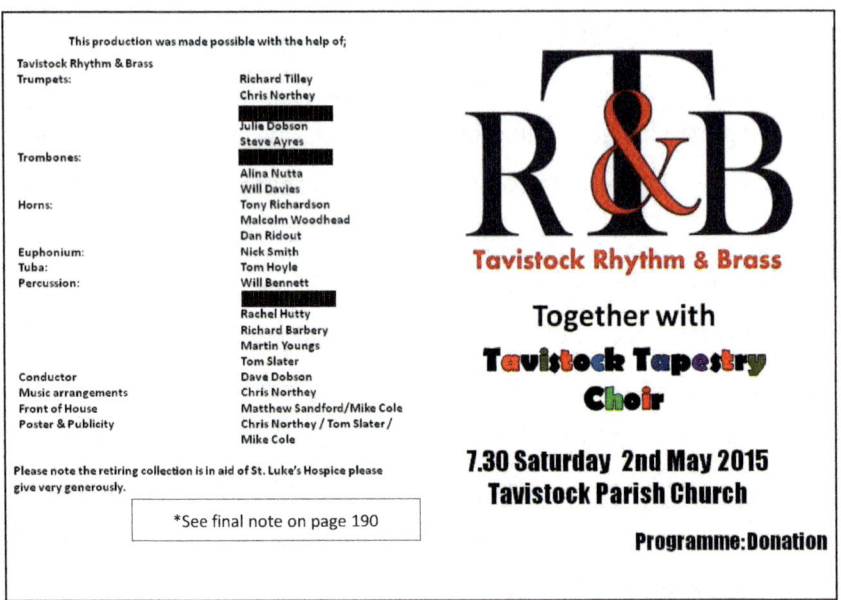

Our 2015 May concert in Tavistock Parish Church, was to be our best yet. It even featured a substantial piece by our favourite composer Brian Balmages. It, not only, included all our percussion, [in the extreme], but also parts for grand piano and a full choir. This was as far as you could get from a traditional brass band concert.

Since the 2001 move to the Brass Group format, we had not had a formal committee as we felt we managed without one. The group was small, with the same core of players, and any decisions were easily made between us during a rehearsal. We had existed fine with the normal committee roles being taken on by the same members each year. This seemed to work well and had held us in good stead for over fifteen years. Between us, we managed our finances, music library, and inventory of instruments and equipment together with organising concerts, fundraising and charity work. This had produced the band's most stable environment for, perhaps, over a hundred years. We had regular full attendance and everyone seemed happy.

Here we can be seen before our final concert at Tavistock Parish Church 2nd May 2015. *

TR&B Looking good in our newly purchased red shirts, and all with happy faces and smiles. *

It was around this time that a new person asked to join our 'happy band'; we'll call him 'Abaddon' [see footnote on page 195]. He seemed very hands on and keen to help the group, and he was, undoubtedly, a very good musician. He seemed to be a very pleasant person and I had no reason to decline his request. However, a few people said that we should be wary of having him involved in our group and it later turned out he might have even been asked to leave a couple of other bands and some people intimated that an internet search had revealed that he could have, even have been convicted of fraud. [Not my words and I do not endorse these statements].

During one rehearsal it became apparent that, perhaps, we were starting to outgrow our rehearsal premises. The percussion equipment took up a large part of the room and the volume in the room with its heavy thick stone walls was, perhaps a little on the loud side. One night a part of the ceiling came crashing down and it was clear that we needed a bigger room for our numbers.

Abaddon took it upon himself to find new rehearsal premises. He had been a 'very hands-on' member since joining a year before and, as a happy welcoming band, we were pleased to bring him into the fold, and within a few weeks we had an additional rehearsal room at a nearby village school. Luckily, they were also happy to store the main bits of percussion equipment which meant we did not have to keep moving items from our Tavistock rehearsal rooms. Abaddon suggested introducing a one-pound membership fee per week, which would act to cover the cost of the school hall premises, and everyone was fine with this suggestion, and so began our new venture with a large rehearsal hall at this local primary school. The playground outside was certainly welcome as it provided plenty of parking, something that was at a premium around our Tavistock rehearsal room.

If you have noticed anything while reading through this brass band's history, it most probably is now, thinking back through what you have already read is that Committees or certain strong individuals or small factions have the power to either maintain transition or destroy potentially volatile groups such as brass bands. Ask any brass band person what the bane of the brass banding world is, they will tell you the first thing is politics and the second is when bands get decimated by families who have a number of its members in a brass band walking out en-bloc. Thirdly it would be committees, who at times make the wrong decision, and finally by players who just want to come along and play.

They turn up, play, and you don't hear from them until the next time the band rehearses. They do not want to get involved in the logistics of keeping a brass band alive, they do not want to be on a Committee and some won't even lift a chair. The whole microcosm of society is to be found in almost every brass band. The potential for almost total annihilation is, often only just around the corner.

Since the transition of the brass band into a brass group, I had taken it upon myself to keep the band's history alive and, together with my small team of banding friends, had worked tirelessly to keep our music going in Tavistock with the various reincarnations of Tavistock Town Band. For well over 15 years thousands of pounds had been raised for charity, concerts had been held and music had been made. Who needed a committee?

But, unbeknown to me, Abaddon had been working behind the scenes to bring change to how the Brass Group was run and functioned. At one particular-rehearsal our conductor, Dave Dobson, was made to feel so uncomfortable being questioned and challenged on his conducting skills, which were second to none by the way, that he felt he had no option but to leave the group there and then. This was a sad evening indeed, particularly as it also meant that we lost his wife Julie who was a very competent trumpet and flugel horn player. It was like being transported back in time, to previous unfortunate events. Abaddon was quick to suggest a replacement, and Duncan Newman stood in as Conductor, together with his sister Penny joining on trumpet. Both had played with the band back in the eighties as children, and now as adults came full circle joining Tavistock Rhythm & Brass.

Duncan, no doubt, did his best at conducting the group, but it was clear this was certainly not his forte, and his skills as Master of Ceremonies also lacked finesse. The band worked hard on a programme of new music for a concert at a church in Millbrook, just across the Tamar from Plymouth. This was organised by Abaddon, and because of his promises of his publicity skills being second to none, I was happy to relinquish my usual control. His skills of 'talking the talk' certainly won me over and this was something I was to gravely regret later. He employed the services of a local ladies' barbershop group and choir, and assured us the tickets would fly and that the place would be packed.

On the evening of the concert, all our equipment was transported the substantial distance to the location, and as we arrived at the venue it was clear that we way outnumbered our audience. Our organiser's publicity and promises had failed, dramatically. We also realised that some essential percussion equipment had not turned up and this was later seen, by some members as sabotage, if this was the case, it was a low blow indeed. This was the first time in over fifteen years that people's smiles were being turned upside down. What was going on?

Roche Brass – M.D. Lee Clayson

Malaguena	Mark Freeh	Karl King
Introduction, Act 3, Lohengrin	Richard Wagner	Brian Balmages
An Untold Story (Horn Soloist – Mark Letcher)	Paul Lovatt-Cooper	T L Sharpe
Rolling Thunder	Henry Fillmore	K Anderson – Lopez & R Lopez

Sterts Singers – M.D. Jane Warwick

Run to Me	The Bee Gees #	Robert Sheldon
When The Foeman Bares His Steel	Gilbert and Sullivan	Michael Giacchino
The Long Day Closes	Arthur Sullivan & Henry Chorley	Francis Poulenc
Mr Blue Sky	Jeff Lyne #	Jerome Kern

Tavistock Versatile Brass Ensemble – M.D. Dave Dobson

Curtain Call	John Wasson	Paul Lovatt-Cooper
Freefall	David Shaffer	Trad.
In Your Dreams (Trumpet Soloist – Chris Northey)	Paul Clark	Johann Strauss
Ghost Band	Robert W. Smith	
Happy	Pharrell Williams	Henry Wood
The Wizard of Oz	Harold Arlen	Thomas Arne

Tavistock Versatile Brass Ensemble

Rough Riders (March)		Karl King
Endless Rainbows		Brian Balmages
Blades of Toledo		T L Sharpe
Let it Go (from Disney's "Frozen")		K Anderson – Lopez & R Lopez
Star Trek – Into Darkness		Michael Giacchino
Crazy for Cartoons		Robert Sheldon

Kate Walker

Les chemins de L'amour		Francis Poulenc
All the things you are		Jerome Kern

Roche Brass

Enter the Galaxies		Paul Lovatt-Cooper
Shenandoah		Trad.
Radetsky March		Johann Strauss

Finale

Pomp & Circumstance March No.1 in D (Land of Hope & Glory)		Edward Elgar
Fantasia on British Sea Songs		Henry Wood
Rule Britannia (Soloist – Kate Walker)		Thomas Arne
Jerusalem		Hubert Parry

Please be upstanding for the National Anthem

2014 'Last Night of the Proms' concert at Sterts Theatre, Upton Cross, Bodmin

Chapter 21 – Conclusion

"Having things taken away from you is not the same as giving them away." – **Paula Gosling** – American Crime Writer

Like lots of brass bands all over the country and even the world, many bands struggle to make it into the history books or even their own history books. Bands and groups come and go without leaving a single mark on history. Brilliant concerts, music, dance; fireworks and pyrotechnics, lighting effects and displays fade into history and are forgotten. Tavistock Town Band had done well to survive over one hundred years and beyond. Yes, of course, people will always come and go. They move away for further education or they or their families move for work and, of course, unfortunately, good players and friends pass away. Even in just my short forty years with Tavistock, I had seen much of this over the years. Our previous training bands and academies rarely produce players for our bands, but instead for someone else's as they moved to other parts of the country and even the world. But, we were, also, lucky enough to occasionally gain from people moving into our area who had gained brass band training elsewhere – you see it can occasionally work both ways.

Unfortunately, schools now struggle to provide musical instrument tuition, and the days of having a plethora of school bands and orchestras is something that only private schools seem able to provide. Much emphasis is given to science and sport, rather than the arts and music. Unfortunately, British schools are so far removed from schools in some other countries, and it seems that we are now forgetting what we once had. My friends in America are amazed that not everyone is given the opportunity to gain from the benefits of playing a musical instrument during their school days. A study by Sheffield University in 2019 concluded categorically that playing in a brass band can improve your health and mental well-being. The research found that being part of a brass band can enhance people's physical, psychological, social, emotional and even spiritual health. Playing in a brass band can help improve some respiratory conditions and have similar mental cleansing effects to meditating. Brass banding can also help to reduce stress, increase resilience and improve mental health. With so much of the resources of our NHS being consumed due to mental health issues, perhaps Doctors should start prescribing taking up a brass instrument and joining a brass band?

But even when you think you have a stable group of friends and playing members things can all too easily be changed and taken away. At a meeting of Tavistock Rhythm & Brass in 2015, a couple of new members led by Abaddon decided that a committee was the way forward in running the group. They had worked hard behind the scenes on their coup d'état to bring their idea to even the most long-standing members of the group. The 'brainwashing' was complete. Abaddon had shown his true colours. No longer would the main decisions over music programmes, concerts, fundraising, charity work and instrument allocation go to just one person or even a couple of people, but a whole new Committee would be formed and they had decided that I would not be part of it. After being in the band for forty years I was now being thrown out of my own band.

The remaining group [I was told] failed dramatically at their last ever Concert at Sterts theatre, the following September.

I now found myself in that difficult position that many key people in Tavistock Town Band's history had faced previously. Having been in the band continually since 1976, I now found it was time to walk away. I had seen previously the destruction committees and certain egotistical people had done, and given the hold of a few new members over the nucleus of the group, the demise of Tavistock's Town Band was secured. As it turned out, I was moving away from the Tavistock area anyway, much like a number of those kids who had learnt their instrument skills in our training bands previously. I would not be around to see the final failure. I removed all my music arrangements and personally purchased music from the Brass Group library, returned my instrument, uniform, and rehearsal room keys and left.

Some of my so-called friends remained in the resulting brass group until the September, when at our annual 'Last Night of the Proms' concert at the Sterts Theatre, Upton Cross, on the edge of Bodmin Moor, Cornwall, they tried to reproduce our previous evening spectacle. My heart lifted when I found out, one member listened to his conscience and after setting up the timpani drums, walked out, and did not take part in the concert. Feedback from the concert was that it was a total failure. [Their words not mine]. The music programme seemed under rehearsed and poorly performed. They did not join with a full brass band to perform the normal roof raising finale items of 'Rule Britannia', 'Sea Songs', 'Jerusalem' and 'Land of Hope & Glory'. Reports were that the group struggled to play the finale pieces and the atmosphere was simply not the same as in previous years. They had employed the services of an Irish Dance troop and a Magician, in an effort to fill the programme. I'm not trying to 'blow my own trumpet' [again excuse the pun] but I had always been Master of Ceremonies and had incorporated audience participation and good humour to fill the gaps between musical items or guest soloists, and the feedback I received was "things were simply not the same". Unsurprisingly, Abaddon and his group were not asked to return for the following year.

I have been told; the remaining Brass Group lasted less than 12 months before folding completely. Abaddon and his committee struggled to find new rehearsal rooms after being asked to leave the school premises. They had previously told the Tavistock Council that they no longer needed the basement rehearsal space and this was quickly 'snapped up' by the town's Tavistock Musical Theatre Company for storage and rehearsal. Some members, who subsequently got in touch to apologise for their lack of support at the 'meeting' have advised that things very quickly went downhill after I left. They now had nowhere to store the large amounts of percussion equipment, and all but one percussionist had left the group anyway. The group tried several Plymouth rehearsal premises, but found no suitable ongoing locations that were willing to store the large amount of equipment. By losing the Tavistock premises they really had 'cut off their noses'. They tried to re-launch their group a few times and changed the name, again, to 'Blow Zone'. Ultimately, it appears that they had their own 'snow ball effect'.

Just when you thought Abaddon and his cohorts had done enough to bring sadness to Tavistock's banding history; they still had a final personal attack up their sleeve. They made an accusation to the Police that I had stolen band funds totalling nearly ten thousand pounds. They accused me of reimbursing myself as Treasurer after, apparently, pretending to purchase instruments and equipment to that sum and then, that I had pocketed the money. They claimed I had no receipts to justify the reimbursements. As the new equipment was purchased online, I had to use my own personal credit card to make the purchases. I then reimbursed myself for the amounts concerned. I was summoned to Tavistock police station and interviewed under caution. Of course, I was able to produce receipts for all the amounts I had claimed and explained that the band had the said assets in their possession. All accusations against me were of course dismissed by the investigating Police Officer.

Final Note

"If it ain't broke – don't fix it" – **Thomas Bertram Lance** – *Director of the Office of Management and Budget in US President Jimmy Carter's 1977 administration.*

Sadly, it now appears [2023] that no remnant of Tavistock Town Band or any such brass group remains. Even the last few remaining players who were willing to talk to me about the group's demise, have not been able to confirm what happened to the extensive collection of expensive assets. Even at a second-hand price, their value would in excess of ten thousand pounds. No one seems willing to confirm their location - or have they already been sold? Only one person knows – and Abaddon is 'not telling'.

This time, it appears the Tavistock Town Council were not asked to store the instruments, assets and substantial monetary funds. Therefore, it seems this is where the history of Tavistock Town Band sadly concludes.

* Note the identities and images of the Abaddon team have been blurred and obscured, their names and identities are not revealed or implied to persons living or deceased.

Footnote – Who Is Abaddon?

The term 'abaddon' appears in the Bible as both a place of destruction and an angel of the abyss. In the Hebrew Bible 'Abaddon' is used with reference to a bottomless pit, often appearing alongside the place Sheol, meaning the resting place of dead people. In the Book of Revelations of the New Testament, an angel called Abaddon is described as the King of an army of locusts; his name is first transcribed in Koine Greek – Revelation 9:11 – "Whose name in Hebrew is **Abaddon – the Destroyer**"

R.I.P. – Tavistock Town Band 1897 – 2015

ABOUT THE AUTHOR

Christopher H. Northey-Youngs was born and grew up in the Westcountry market town of Tavistock in Devon, and from an early age found a passion for music and making people 'smile'. He learnt piano and trumpet at an early age and although the arts and creativity beckoned as a possible career, he found himself working for a Bank for thirty years followed by eight years as a Funeral Director and mortuary worker. To compensate for an outlet for his creativity and sense of fun, Chris had many leading roles in theatrical productions, and also played trumpet in a 'swing band', [Raymon Hale Singers & Swing South West]. He played French horn and trumpet in Plymouth University Orchestra, and on many occasions he played the Last Post at Tavistock's Armistice Day Parade and Service. He helped friends in their brass bands, taught piano and music theory, and of course enjoyed his own personal passion, his brass group, for which he did hundreds of bespoke music arrangements. Chris always tries to follow his personal mantra, "educate and entertain".

Printed in Dunstable, United Kingdom